T0318907

Cambridge Elements ≡

Elements in Earth System Governance
edited by
Frank Biermann
Utrecht University
Aarti Gupta
Wageningen University
Michael Mason
London School of Economics and Political Science

TRADE
AND THE ENVIRONMENT

*Drivers and Effects of Environmental
Provisions in Trade Agreements*

Clara Brandi
*German Institute of Development
and Sustainability (IDOS)*

Jean-Frédéric Morin
Laval University

CAMBRIDGE
UNIVERSITY PRESS

Shaftesbury Road, Cambridge CB2 8EA, United Kingdom

One Liberty Plaza, 20th Floor, New York, NY 10006, USA

477 Williamstown Road, Port Melbourne, VIC 3207, Australia

314–321, 3rd Floor, Plot 3, Splendor Forum, Jasola District Centre, New Delhi – 110025, India

103 Penang Road, #05–06/07, Visioncrest Commercial, Singapore 238467

Cambridge University Press is part of Cambridge University Press & Assessment, a department of the University of Cambridge.

We share the University's mission to contribute to society through the pursuit of education, learning and research at the highest international levels of excellence.

www.cambridge.org
Information on this title: www.cambridge.org/9781009461870

DOI: 10.1017/9781009461825

First published 2023

A catalogue record for this publication is available from the British Library

ISBN 978-1-009-46187-0 Hardback
ISBN 978-1-009-46183-2 Paperback
ISSN 2631-7818 (online)
ISSN 2631-780X (print)

Cambridge University Press & Assessment has no responsibility for the persistence or accuracy of URLs for external or third-party internet websites referred to in this publication and does not guarantee that any content on such websites is, or will remain, accurate or appropriate.

Trade and the Environment

Drivers and Effects of Environmental Provisions in Trade Agreements

Elements in Earth System Governance

DOI: 10.1017/9781009461825
First published online: December 2023

Clara Brandi
German Institute of Development and Sustainability (IDOS)

Jean-Frédéric Morin
Laval University

Author for correspondence: Prof. Dr. Clara Brandi,
Clara.Brandi@idos-research.de

Abstract: The mushrooming of trade agreements and their interlinkages with environmental governance calls for new research on the trade and environment interface. The more than 700 existing preferential trade agreements (PTAs) include ever more diverse and far-reaching environmental provisions. While missed opportunities remain and harmful provisions persist, numerous environmental provisions in PTAs entail promising potential. They promote the implementation of environmental treaties and cover numerous environmental issues. New concepts, data, and methods, including detailed content analysis across multiple institutions, are needed to explain these interlinkages and understand whether and how PTAs with environmental provisions can contribute to tackling global environmental challenges. Making use of the most extensive coding of environmental provisions in PTAs to date and combining quantitative data with qualitative analyses, this Element provides a comprehensive yet fine-grained picture of the drivers and effects of environmental provisions in PTAs. This title is also available as Open Access on Cambridge Core.

This Element also has a video abstract: www.cambridge.org/Brandi

Keywords: trade agreements, environmental governance, regime complex, interlinkages, earth system governance

ISBNs: 9781009461870 (HB), 9781009461832 (PB), 9781009461825 (OC)
ISSNs: 2631-7818 (online), 2631-780X (print)

Contents

1 Introduction

The Challenges of Multilateral Governance

In 2015, the global community achieved two significant milestones in multilateralism: the Paris Agreement and the 2030 Agenda for Sustainable Development. The Paris Agreement aims to limit the increase in global temperature to below 2° C above pre-industrial levels, with a preference for staying below 1.5°C (UNFCCC, 2015). The 2030 Agenda is centred around seventeen sustainable development goals (SDGs), designed to address the three pillars of sustainability: social, environmental, and economic (United Nations, 2015).[1]

Despite these notable accomplishments, global cooperation is facing tremendous pressure. The progress of multilateral climate negotiations towards implementing the Paris Agreement has been frustratingly slow. Other multilateral approaches dealing with global environmental challenges are also progressing at a sluggish pace, such as the global biodiversity regime or non-existent altogether, as in the case of ocean acidification.

At the same time, multilateral trade negotiations at the World Trade Organization (WTO) have encountered significant obstacles. While there have been some recent breakthroughs,[2] it has been nearly three decades since the conclusion of the last major multilateral trade agreement. The WTO has become a victim of its own success (Baldwin, 2010), as the focus shifted from reducing tariffs to aligning domestic regulatory approaches (Hoekman, 2014). With an increasing number of heterogeneous members, reaching a consensus on multilateral solutions has become more challenging, resulting in the 'legislative gridlock' of the WTO (Narlikar, 2010). The Doha Round negotiations, which aimed to address the concerns of developing countries, reached an impasse with no resolution in sight. Furthermore, the rise of new economic powers such as China and India has made achieving global consensus even more challenging than before (Hale et al., 2013). Populism, trade wars, and ongoing military conflicts continue to undermine global economic cooperation.

Nevertheless, policy actions are necessary. Human interference in the Earth's system has reached an unprecedented scale, posing enormous challenges for scientists and policymakers that call for global cooperation and a shift towards sustainability. We are now in the Anthropocene, a new geological age in which humans are altering the very Earth system upon which our livelihoods depend.

---

[1] Because of their broad coverage, the Paris Agreement and the 2030 Agenda have the potential to favour 'catalytic cooperation' by incrementally changing the preferences of various actors (Hale, 2020).

[2] For example, after multiple years of negotiations, the WTO Agreement on Fisheries Subsidies was finally adopted in 2022.

Global economic governance cannot remain stagnant in the face of these existential challenges.

The Importance of Studying the Trade and Environment Interplay

This Element explores the complex and contested relationship between trade governance and environmental governance by analysing its drivers and effects. Understanding this relationship is critical for several reasons: First, international trade is integral to the modern world economy. We cannot understand our patterns of resource extraction and consumption without examining how and why these resources travel across borders. The value of exports has increased more than forty times since 1913. This increase was even more pronounced than the global production growth. Not only do we produce more goods but we also export a greater share of what we produce.

Second, international trade has significant environmental impacts. For instance, carbon emissions embodied in trade constitute a large and growing share of global emissions (Sato, 2014). The harmful effects of air pollution on Chinese residents, for example, are primarily associated with exports to the United States (US) (Wiedmann & Lenzen, 2018). Moreover, between 29 per cent and 39 per cent of deforestation-related emissions are driven by international trade, mainly in beef and oilseeds like palm oil (Pendrill et al., 2019). The United Kingdom (UK), Germany, France, Italy, and Japan 'imported' more than 90 per cent of their national deforestation footprints from abroad between 2001 and 2015, of which between 46 per cent and 57 per cent were from tropical forests (Hoang & Kanemoto, 2021). Thus, trade is highly relevant from an environmental perspective. The stakes are particularly high for developing countries because the harmful effects of trade are concentrated in the Global South.

Third, trade can contribute to addressing environmental problems (for more details, see Section 2). Trade can enable more resource-efficient production, the spread of environmental standards, and the diffusion of environmentally friendly technologies. Given these mixed effects, it is not surprising that the relationship between trade and the environment remains controversial. Debates on the positive and negative effects of trade on the environment were particularly heated during the negotiations for the Transatlantic Trade and Investment Partnership (TTIP) between the US and the European Union (EU) and the negotiations between the EU and the Mercosur countries, Argentina, Brazil, Paraguay, and Uruguay.

Fourth, the design of trade policies matters for environmental protection. In some cases, trade policies have been poorly designed. For example, import tariffs and nontariff barriers tend to be lower in dirty industries than in clean industries, creating a global implicit subsidy for CO_2 emissions (Shapiro, 2021). If countries applied similar trade policies to clean and dirty goods, global CO_2 emissions would decrease by 1 per cent to 5 per cent, which is comparable to the estimated effects of the European Union Emissions Trading System (Shapiro, 2021). Conversely, well-designed preferential trade agreements (PTAs) can have beneficial environmental effects. For example, PTAs with environmental provisions can increase the export of environmental goods by 17 per cent (Brandi et al., 2020) and reduce forest losses by an average of approximately 23 per cent (Abman et al., 2021).

Finally, analysing the interplay between trade and the environment is vital in the context of the modern global governance system, which is characterized by a complex web of institutions with overlapping mandates. The age of siloed global governance is over. Today, international agreements do not develop in isolation from one another, as was initially assumed by the earlier regime theory and some of the treaty design literature. Instead, institutions interact with each other and are typically embedded in a broader regime complex (Raustiala & Victor, 2004). The interface between international regimes must be addressed directly to tackle current urgent global challenges with limited resources. Previous research on the interlinkages between trade and the environment has primarily focused on the WTO. This Element contributes to a more recent generation of scholarship that considers novel ways to link trade and the environment in bilateral and regional trade agreements.

Looking at Preferential Trade Agreements and Their Environmental Provisions

In this Element, we focus on exploring the potential contribution of PTAs to global environmental governance. Since 1947, over 770 PTAs have been concluded, with increasingly diverse and far-reaching environmental provisions. Although missed opportunities and harmful provisions still exist, numerous environmental provisions within PTAs have great potential. Some provisions promote the implementation of environmental treaties, facilitate civil society participation, and require the transfer of environmental technologies to developing countries. These provisions cover a wide range of environmental issues, such as limiting deforestation, protecting fish stocks, and mitigating CO_2 emissions. Additionally, some PTAs provide for the use of their primary dispute settlement mechanisms, which can ultimately lead to trade sanctions in cases of alleged non-compliance with environmental provisions.

The proliferation of PTAs and their environmental provisions necessitates new research on the trade-environment interface. New data and methods, including detailed content analysis across multiple treaties, are needed to explain the interlinkages and understand if and how PTAs' environmental provisions can help tackle global environmental challenges.

While acknowledging the challenges and negative externalities resulting from tensions between the trade and environmental regimes, this Element asks a different question: How can trade governance be part of the solution and strengthen environmental governance? Our investigation aims to determine whether, why, and how PTAs can contribute to environmental protection.

Overall, this Element demonstrates that well-designed environmental provisions within trade agreements can improve environmental protection and promote the SDGs.

The Element addresses four key questions that are explored throughout its sections:

1. How does global governance at the trade-environment interface contribute to environmental performance? The Element demonstrates that global governance at the trade-environment interface can mitigate the negative externalities of trade and increase positive externalities. This indicates that international institutions really do matter, which is a useful reminder in these troubled times as they are increasingly being attacked by nationalists and populists, as well as cynical and disillusioned activists.
2. To what extent does governance at the trade-environment interface lead to trade-offs between the economic and environmental dimensions of sustainable development? While governing the trade-environment interface may create trade-offs, it can also create synergies across the different dimensions of sustainable development. For example, environmental provisions that reduce trade barriers for environmental goods can generate economic and environmental benefits.
3. To what extent do high-income countries take advantage of power imbalances to impose their views on the trade-environment interface? The Element recognizes the power dynamics in international relations and emphasizes the need for environmental provisions to be designed in a way that considers the interests of developing countries and their most vulnerable populations.
4. As more environmental provisions are included in more trade agreements, what are the implications for the fragmented nature of trade and environment interlinkages and regime complexes? The Element acknowledges the challenges posed by the fragmentation of global governance architecture (Bhagwati, 2008; Biermann, 2014; Young, 2012), particularly in terms of

coordination and coherence. Fragmentation also creates opportunities for innovation and adaptability (Abbott, 2014; Faude, 2020; Gehring & Faude, 2014; Jinnah, 2011; Oberthür & Gehring, 2006). This Element contributes to this second line of inquiry. The inclusion of environmental provisions in PTAs provides a framework for experimenting with trade-environment interlinkages and can potentially help to overcome the stalemate in the WTO. This Element suggests that this can enhance the adaptability of the global trade system to pressing environmental challenges.

Data and Methods

This Element synthesizes our previous research on the interplay between trade and the environment. Its originality lies in the analysis of an update version of the TRade and ENvironment Database (TREND), the most comprehensive dataset of its kind.[3] The original version of TREND released in 2018 covered 670 PTAs concluded between 1947 and 2016 (Morin et al., 2018b). This updated version of TREND includes over 100 additional PTAs and provides the latest insights into the content and design of these agreements.[4]

Using a dataset as large and detailed as TREND offers numerous analytical benefits. It enables us to draw generalizable lessons beyond the idiosyncrasies of controversial trade agreements. Moreover, using large-n datasets makes it possible to use statistical techniques to uncover causal effects, for example, those based on panel data analysis or the quasi-experimental method of propensity score matching. Various robustness tests can be used to substantiate the empirical findings. Furthermore, large-n approaches offer an important birds-eye perspective on the issue, analysing the global governance architecture of trade and the environment across the full spectrum of PTAs (Biermann & Kim, 2020).

To complement the use of quantitative approaches, this Element relies on qualitative research methods and includes insights gained from semi-structured interviews. We conducted nine interviews with trade officials and other experts, among others from the EU, the US, Chile, and New Zealand (see Annex). The interviews were conducted via telephone or video calls, transcribed, and analysed. The semi-structured interviews included several questions focusing on trade and environment interlinkage in the context of the negotiations of PTAs, their implementation, and post-agreement cooperation.

---

[3] As the original version of TREND, the update builds on the collection of PTAs maintained by DESTA. See Dür et al. (2014).

[4] The data can be explored using TREND Analytics (www.TRENDanalytics.info), an interactive online data tool that makes this data more accessible beyond the academic community (Berger et al., 2017). Otherwise, the dataset is available in Excel format at www.trend.ulaval.ca.

By combining these diverse research methods, we aim to provide a comprehensive and detailed understanding of the interlinkages between trade and environmental governance.

Our Contribution

In contrast to the prevailing perspective that the fragmentation of the trading system has only negative consequences (Bhagwati, 1995), our Element argues that the fragmentation of trade and environmental governance can be seen more positively and can be regarded, under certain conditions, as productive in terms of environmental protection. In some cases, the dynamism of the trade regime complex has become a leverage point for environmental protection. Therefore, this Element offers a foundation for enhancing the readiness of current trade governance systems to address urgent global environmental challenges and Earth system transformations such as climate change and biodiversity loss.

This argument is significant and relevant, because the relationship between trade and the environment has become increasingly important. The issue of whether and how to link trade and the environment in PTAs is a highly debated topic in both research and policy circles. For instance, major disputes have recently arisen in the context of the EU-Mercosur trade agreement and the WTO agenda on trade and the environment. Furthermore, the introduction of a carbon border adjustment mechanism (CBAM) by the EU – a tariff on carbon-intensive EU imports – has sparked further contentious discussions about trade and environmental linkages. Drawing on insights from law, economics, and political science, this Element provides a comprehensive investigation of the governance of the trade-environment interface in the light of the proliferation of environmental provisions in PTAs.

This Element contributes to Earth System Governance (ESG) research and the Science and Implementation plan. Above all, it relates to the ESG research lens 'Architecture and Agency', which focuses on 'understanding the institutional frameworks and actors implicated in earth system governance and how these institutions and actors resist or respond to change and evolve over time' (Burch et al., 2019). Consistent with the ESG research plan, this Element places a special emphasis on governance architecture as 'the interlocking web of widely shared principles, institutions, and practices that shape decisions at all levels in a given area of earth system governance' (Biermann et al., 2009a, p. 31). This Element contributes to the discussion on three topics that are particularly salient in the context of architecture issues: institutional interlinkages, regime complexity, and fragmentation.

The Element is organized as follows. Section 2 examines the proliferation of PTAs and their environmental provisions in the context of institutional interlinkages, regime complexes, and fragmentation. Section 3 introduces trade and environmental interlinkages, explores the diverse environmental provisions found in PTAs, and discusses their compliance and enforcement mechanisms. Section 4 investigates the various drivers of PTA environmental provisions, which are becoming increasingly frequent and diverse. Section 5 explores the important North-South dynamics of PTA negotiations and the inclusion of environmental provisions. Section 6 examines the global spread of environmental provisions in PTAs. Section 7 analyses the effects of environmental provisions in PTAs from both environmental and economic perspectives, examining the synergies and trade-offs between different dimensions of sustainable development. Section 8 goes beyond the bilateral and regional levels and considers broader implications for greening trade governance at the multilateral level. Section 9 summarizes the potential benefits and pitfalls of environmental provisions in trade agreements and presents ten evidence-based policy recommendations.

Overall, this Element provides a comprehensive and nuanced analysis of the relationship between trade and the environment in the context of PTAs, drawing on both quantitative and qualitative research methods to offer insights into the drivers, effects, and implications of environmental provisions in trade agreements.

2 Trade and Environment: Interlinkages, Complexity, and Fragmentation

In the early 2000s, the global governance literature shifted its attention from distinct international institutions to the growing interlinkages between them (Raustiala & Victor, 2004). As new interrelated issues came to the forefront, numerous institutions were created, leading to a progressively crowded global governance landscape. The resulting interconnections generated larger complexes of interacting institutions. Ultimately, they gave rise to governance architectures, that is, 'overarching system of public and private institutions, principles, norms, regulations, decision-making procedures and organizations that are valid or active in a given area of global governance' (Biermann & Kim, 2020, p. 4). The features of governance architectures are frequently characterized, among other things, in terms of their interlinkages, complexity and fragmentation (Biermann & Kim, 2020). Therefore, we explore the interplay between trade and the environment by investigating *interlinkages* between two *fragmented* sets of institutions, frequently referred to as *regime complexes*.

Institutional Interlinkages

An increasing number of institutions have been established to address novel issues. They interact and form institutional interlinkages, that is, 'formal or informal connections between two institutions and their associated policy processes' (Hickmann et al., 2020, p. 120).[5] The incorporation of environmental provisions into trade agreements is a typical example of institutional interlinkage politics.

In recent decades, institutions and their interactions have mushroomed across global governance architectures. Typologies of institutional interlinkages have also developed rapidly (e.g., Stokke, 2000, 2001; Young, 1996, 2002). The literature on environmental interlinkages has largely focused on 'utilitarian' interlinkages (Stokke, 2001), which are aimed at cost reduction and efficiency. However, recent research indicates that some interlinkages can also be characterized as 'catalytic' (Betsill et al., 2015; Hale, 2020) as they are designed to facilitate action.

Interlinkages can lead to conflicts, synergies, or may be neutral (Oberthür & Gehring, 2006a, p. 46; Pulkowski, 2014; van Asselt, 2014; Zelli, 2010). Although interlinkage conflicts have been conceptualized in different ways (Pulkowski, 2014; van Asselt, 2014), the notion 'remains under-explored' (Hickmann et al., 2020, p. 125). A useful distinction differentiates narrowly defined 'norm conflicts' from broader 'policy conflicts' (van Asselt, 2014). While norm conflicts, that is, incompatibilities between the norms of two treaties, may have some relevance in the context under consideration, we focus on policy conflicts, that is, broader tensions. We explicitly conceptualize these tensions as 'trade-offs'. We show that two interlinked institutions may not only have different goals and be in conflict, but that achieving one institution's goal may only be possible at the expense of the other.

Thereby, we address not only the literature on institutional interlinkages but also the concept of policy coherence, which strives to leverage synergies and minimize trade-offs (OECD, 2019). Surprisingly, synergies have received much less attention in the literature than conflicts (Hickmann et al., 2020). Against this background, our Element seeks to draw attention to trade-offs *and* synergies in relation to trade and environment interlinkages.

While most research on trade and environment interlinkages has focused on the WTO, less attention has been paid to interlinkages in bilateral and regional PTAs, which is the focus of this Element. The majority of existing studies on

---

[5] Interlinkages are also referred to as institutional interactions, institutional interplay, and institutional overlap (e.g., Betsill et al., 2015; Oberthür & Gehring, 2011; Oberthür & Stokke, 2011; Zelli & van Asselt, 2010).

trade and environment interlinkages investigate the WTO (Charnovitz, 2007; Conca, 2000; Eckersley, 2004; Jinnah, 2010, 2014; Johnson, 2015; Neumayer, 2004; Zelli & van Asselt, 2010).[6] Existing scholarship on the environmental provisions of PTAs has largely focused on the North American Free Trade Agreement (NAFTA) and its innovative environmental side agreement (e.g., Gallagher, 2004; Hufbauer, 2000). Some scholarship explores environmental provisions in US PTAs (Jinnah, 2011; Jinnah & Morin, 2020), as well as US and EU perspectives regarding environmental content in PTAs (Bastiaens & Postnikov, 2017; Benson et al., 2022; Jinnah & Morgera, 2013; Morin & Rochette, 2017). However, only a limited number of studies have assessed the environmental provisions in trade agreements across a larger number of PTAs.

Regime Complexes

The proliferation of institutional interlinkages between hundreds and thousands of organizations, agreements, and other institutions in international politics is such that it prompted the development of the concept of 'regime complex' (Abbott, 2012; Alter & Meunier, 2009; Gómez-Mera et al., 2020; Keohane & Victor, 2009; Orsini et al., 2013; Raustiala & Victor, 2004). It is a 'signature feature of twenty-first century international cooperation' (Alter & Raustiala, 2018). A regime complex is a 'network of three or more international regimes that relate to a common subject matter, exhibit overlapping membership, and generate substantive, normative, or operative interactions recognized as potentially problematic whether or not they are managed effectively' (Orsini et al., 2013, p. 29).

In comparison to institutional interlinkages, the concept of regime complex captures the myriad connections between three or more institutions within the context of their broader governance at a more systemic analytical level (Hickmann et al., 2020). As a result of the growing interest in regime complexes, complexity has become a major approach for investigating global governance architectures (Duit et al., 2020; Oberthür & Stokke, 2011; Pattberg & Zelli, 2016).

Fragmentation

Fragmentation is a key feature of global governance architectures and can be defined as the proliferation of actors, institutions, and instruments, which can result in a lack of coordination and coherence among them (Biermann et al., 2009b). Research on fragmentation investigates global governance architectures

---

[6] The WTO is shaping the trade and environment interplay in the framework of its dispute settlement function and various environmental disputes on issues such as solar panels and biofuels (Meyer, 2017; Trachtman, 2018). The WTO's negotiation function also shapes environmental governance; for example, consider the recently concluded negotiations on fishery subsidies.

from the perspective of integration and decentralization (Biermann et al., 2009b; Keohane &Victor, 2011; Zelli & van Asselt, 2013). For instance, it has shed light on how state actors enter partnerships with non-state actors (Pattberg, 2010; Pattberg & Widerberg, 2016) and assessed the increasing role of private governance such as certification (Auld et al., 2015).

More recently, researchers have begun to study potential responses to fragmented governance systems (van Asselt & Zelli, 2014). In the context of the question of how fragmentation can be managed, particular attention is given to the interactions between diverse regimes (Jinnah & Lindsay, 2016; van Asselt, 2014), including those that govern trade and the environment. Possible responses to the fragmentation of governance architectures and their complexity include policy integration, which aims at including environmental goals into non-environmental policy realms, or interplay management, which seeks to restrict conflicts generated by institutional interlinkages (Biermann & Kim, 2020).

Introducing the Trade Regime Complex

The trade regime complex has grown rapidly in recent years, and is still expanding. An increasing number of actors and institutions are interested in governing trade-relevant questions, which has generated a complex governance architecture. A dense regime complex for trade has emerged, featuring numerous overlaps between inter- and transnational institutions. The complex is growing in three ways with regard to: institutions, the issues addressed (including the environment), and geography (developing countries and rising powers are increasingly active players) (Meunier & Morin, 2015).

First, the trade regime complex is expanding on an institutional level. Given the deadlock in multilateral trade negotiations, negotiators are increasingly turning to bilateral and regional trade agreements. More than 700 PTAs have been concluded since 1947. The mushrooming of PTAs can be characterized as 'the main change to the international trading system since the mid-1990s' (Baccini & Dür, 2015, p. 617). As shown in Figure 1, virtually all countries have concluded more than ten PTAs, including the US, China, India, Japan, and most African countries. Moreover, multiple countries are parties to more than fifty PTAs, including Brazil and Mexico. Some countries, particularly in Europe, are party to seventy or more (up to ninety) trade agreements.

The term PTA covers different types of agreements, including sector agreements, free trade areas, custom unions, and common markets. A sectoral agreement is limited to a particular trade issue or sector, such as trade in services or in the automobile sector. A free trade area eliminates tariffs between two or more

Number of PTAs
- 1-9
- 10-29
- 30-49
- 50-69
- 70-89
- 90 +

Figure 1 World map with number of PTAs per country

countries and can also reduce non-tariff barriers to trade on goods and services (e.g., the Regional Comprehensive Economic Partnership or RCEP). A customs union is a special type of free trade area in which the members of the agreement agree to apply a common set of external tariffs to imports from the rest of the world (e.g., the Southern Common Market, MERCOSUR). A common market, in turn, is even more integrated: it not only offers the free movement of goods and services but also the free movement of labour and capital (e.g., the EU). Following the DESTA Project (Dür et al., 2014), the PTAs included in the TREND dataset may be sectoral agreements, free-trade agreements, customs unions, or economic unions.

In addition to PTAs, other institutional forms have developed rapidly in the trade regime complex, including plurilateral agreements (e.g., the Government Procurement Agreement), fora for regulatory agencies (e.g., the International Competition Network), collaboration across intergovernmental organizations (e.g., the Standards and Trade Development Facility) and across private organizations (e.g., the International Accounting Standards Board) (Brandi, 2017).

Second, the trade complex covers an increasing number of issues. It addresses 'WTO-extra' issues, such as tax evasion, which were originally not negotiated in the WTO (Baldwin, 2014; Horn et al., 2010). As these issues are now tackled by a growing number of trade-related initiatives, the scope of the trade regime complex continues to expand.

Traditionally, PTAs aimed to eliminate tariffs, but they now incorporate non-economic policy areas such as the environment. The content of PTAs is gradually diversifying. This can be illustrated by a measure of their depth, which depicts the extent of tariff liberalization and cooperation in the areas of services trade, investments, public procurement, competition, and intellectual

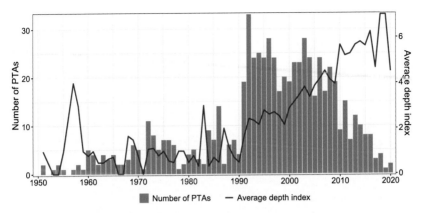

Figure 2 Bar chart with number of PTAs per year and average score of DESTA depth

property rights (Dür et al., 2014).[7] As shown in Figure 2, the average depth of PTAs has risen steadily over the past four decades, indicating the ever-more far-reaching content of PTAs. At the same time, while the average PTA has deepened, some agreements remain shallow. For example, the EU and NAFTA are much deeper agreements than the Association of Southeast Asian Nations (ASEAN) and the Economic Community of West African States (ECOWAS). This heterogeneity is a crucial dimension of the trade agreement landscape.

Third, the trade regime complex is growing geographically. Until the 1990s, only a few countries have been negotiating PTA. However, now-adays, many countries are simultaneously involved in trade negotiations worldwide. The trade complex is an expanding system that can be analysed as a whole (Meunier & Morin, 2015; Pauwelyn & Alschner, 2015).

Implications of Fragmentation and Complexity?

Scholars and decision-makers are concerned that the mushrooming of PTAs will undermine the trade regime, by making the trade system ever more fragmented (Hoeckman & Sabel, 2019), with the so-called spaghetti bowl of PTAs (Bhagwati, 1995, p. 5). Critics argue that PTAs, like termites, eat 'away at the multilateral trading system relentlessly' (Bhagwati, 2008, p. vii). However, PTAs have circumvented this WTO deadlock. They enable subsets of WTO

---

[7] While the indicator does not capture the extent of environmental provisions, it is highly correlated with it (correlation coefficient of roughly 0.9).

members to find consensus on new trade rules where the entire community of WTO members has failed. Preferential trade agreements allow legislative progress and may have the capacity to help the trade order adapt to shifting contexts. Therefore, PTAs can strengthen resilience (Faude, 2020). As we will argue in Section 8, PTAs can also help to promote agreement on new trade rules at the multilateral level, as they can provide a laboratory for experimenting with new rules that can eventually be adopted more widely.

The question of how to evaluate the growing density of overlapping institutions from a normative point of view has received little attention thus far (Hickmann et al., 2020). Regime complexes have both positive and negative effects. They can create winners and losers (Alter & Raustiala, 2018). A regime complex offers substantial benefits; for example, it can enable experimentation, help overcome gridlock, balance deviating societal interests, allow for flexibility, favour innovation, adapt to a changing environment, and facilitate cost and burden sharing (De Búrca et al., 2014; Faude, 2020; Faude & Große-Kreul, 2020; Gehring & Faude, 2013; Pauwelyn, 2014). On the other hand, complex systems involving multiple institutions can also generate challenges: duplication and confusion, substantial knowledge and capacity are required, and institutional interactions must be managed (Biermann et al., 2009b). This tends to privilege those with greater resources (Alter & Raustiala, 2018).

Overall, the impact of fragmentation and complexity on global governance is a topic of debate among scholars (for a comprehensive overview, refer to Biermann & Kim, 2020). Some scholars hold a pessimistic view of fragmented governance structures due to the difficulties of achieving coordination and coherence across various institutions (Biermann, 2014; Young, 2012). However, other scholars are more optimistic about the proliferation of regime complexes and their potential outcomes. They argue that such structures can be more adaptable across time and issue areas than more integrated architectures (Faude, 2020; Keohane & Victor, 2011).

In this Element, we substantiate the optimistic perspective while recognizing the negative aspects of fragmentation. As we will demonstrate, the fragmentation of regime complexes has the potential to enhance the resilience and adaptability of global governance, and can act as a catalyst for environmental protection, provided that it is navigated with caution.

3 Linking Trade and the Environment in PTAs

The relationship between international trade and environmental protection is complex and multi-faceted. There is an ongoing debate, both theoretically and empirically, about whether trade contributes to environmental degradation or helps address environmental challenges. This section aims to outline the current controversies surrounding the relationship between trade and the environment as well as recent trends in the governance of this interplay.[8] Additionally, we highlight the growing diversity of trade agreements and the numerous environmental provisions they contain, along with their various compliance mechanisms.

Trade: Good or Bad for the Environment?

Based on the economic theory of comparative advantage (Ricardo, 1817), some economists argue that international trade increases countries' overall welfare, which in turn enhances environmental protection and provides more affordable access to environmentally friendly goods and services (Bhagwati, 1993). Others describe the relationship between trade and the environment as divergent (Conca, 2000; Esty, 1994). There are serious concerns that more international trade implies more transport and production, and thus, higher resource use and heavier environmental degradation (Daly, 1993).

In 1991, Grossman and Krueger published their seminal paper on how international trade can impact the environment by affecting the scale of economic activity (scale effect), composition of production across industries (composition effect), and emission intensity of individual industries (technique effect). A remarkable discovery was made based on their empirical analysis: international trade may not necessarily have a negative impact on the environment (Grossman & Krueger, 1991).[9]

Although there have been considerable strides in understanding the relationship between trade and the environment by now, there is still a dearth of empirical evidence concerning this interplay and the link between international trade and environmental consequences remains contested (for recent reviews, see Cherniwchan et al., 2017; Cherniwchan & Taylor, 2022). Some studies have found that trade is detrimental to the environment. For example, evidence suggests that international trade is a major source of air pollution in the shipping sector (Gallagher, 2005). Other studies find that trade is good for the environment, for example, by providing evidence that exporting to the EU and the US strengthens environmental performance in developing countries because the consumer demand for environmentally friendly goods and

---

[8] This Element focuses on PTAs and their interlinkages with the environment. At the same time, transnational governance also raises important questions at the trade-environment interface. For example, consider the importance of trade for the diffusion of private sector-led environmental initiatives (Prakash & Potoski, 2006).

[9] By now, research has established that the technique effect is the principal force behind countries' lower pollution levels, but there is still inadequate evidence regarding the role of trade for this technique effect (Cherniwchan & Taylor, 2022).

services in the EU and the US is greater than in developing countries (Gamso, 2017). While some scholars argue that international trade leads to a race to the lowest environmental standards (Daly, 1993), others illustrate that trade can induce the spread of higher environmental standards (Vogel, 2009).

Given these ambiguous findings regarding international trade and environmental protection, it is unclear how their interplay affects the environment. Recent research on the trade-environment interface underlines the importance of the design of trade policies in this regard (Brandi et al., 2020; Shapiro, 2021). It is also unclear how international trade affects sustainable development more broadly. It is frequently argued that trade can be a powerful tool for achieving the SDGs (e.g., Bellmann & Tipping, 2015). Trade can enhance productivity, generate higher incomes, increase growth, and help alleviate poverty (Baccini, 2019; Baier & Bergstrand, 2007; Winters & Martuscelli, 2014). Thus, reducing trade barriers can contribute to achieving several SDGs, including those related to poverty (SDG 1) and growth (SDG 8). Simultaneously, reducing trade barriers always generates winners and losers, and tends to increase inequalities (which contradicts SDG 10). If trade-offs exist between trade and environmental protection, liberalizing trade could undermine the environmental dimensions of sustainable development, making it harder to achieve goals that aim to minimize the use of natural resources (SDG 12) or protect ecosystems, such as forests (SDG 15).

In summary, there are multiple theoretical perspectives on the debate about trade and the environment. However, additional empirical evidence is required to determine whether and how international trade causes environmental problems or whether it can be a solution for tackling growing environmental challenges.

Trade Governance and Environmental Governance

Recently, the use of trade rules as instruments for promoting environmental protection has generated considerable interest. One reason is that environmental agreements have several weaknesses that cast doubt on their capacity to tackle global environmental challenges, even though the number of environmental agreements is increasing. Global environmental governance seeks to make progress based on consensus, which tends to lead to agreements that lack ambition and capacity to overcome pertinent environmental problems (Susskind & Ali, 2014). Moreover, most global environmental agreements lack strong enforcement mechanisms, which can undermine compliance and lead to free riding. Given the weaknesses of global environmental governance, other avenues for environmental protection are being pursued.

Conventionally, trade and the environment used to be governed by distinct regimes. At the same time, attempts to link trade and environmental governance have been underway for decades. This has led to increasing overlap and interactions between different regimes (e.g., Johnson, 2015; Zelli et al., 2013). In recent years, there has been a remarkable shift in the development of novel ways to link trade with the environment. Trade agreements concluded at the bilateral or regional level are central to this development.

Environmental provisions have become a regular feature of PTAs. PTAs offer several advantages over multilateral environmental agreements (MEAs) in terms of negotiating environmental obligations: they reduce the number of players around the negotiation table, facilitate trade-offs across diverse issue areas, are associated with established practices to ensure compliance and enforcement (see also Box 1), and the political involvement of heads of government can help break deadlocks and accelerate the negotiation process. As a result, some PTA environmental provisions set obligations that are more specific, more stringent, and characterized by better enforceability than those contained in environmental agreements.

The Increasing Number of Environmental Provisions

More than 86 per cent of all PTAs include environmental provisions (Morin et al., 2018b). As shown in Figure 3, almost all new PTAs systematically incorporate environmental provisions (with the recent exception of the 2020 sectoral agreement between Brazil and Paraguay).

As depicted in Figure 4, the average number of environmental provisions in PTAs has increased over time.[10] Between 2015 and 2020, each new PTA had an average of forty-eight environmental provisions, illustrating the proliferation of environmental provisions in the trade regime complex. Recent PTAs often include more than 100 environmental provisions. In 2019, the signing of the Agreement between the US, Mexico, and Canada (USMCA), often referred to as NAFTA 2.0, broke a new record: this PTA has 153 environmental provisions.

Substantial variation subsists in the average number of environmental provisions per PTA (see also Baker, 2021). American trade agreements include an average of forty-nine environmental provisions. European PTAs include an average of twenty-six environmental provisions. The difference between US and EU average is chiefly due to the fact that several European PTAs have been concluded in the 1970s, 1980s, and 1990s, before the number of environmental provisions per PTAs took off around the world. In Asia, environmental

---

[10] In the interactive online visualization of TREND (www.TRENDanalytics.info), it is possible to investigate a timeline, geographical patterns, key issues (e.g., climate change) and real-word examples for different types of environmental content in PTAs.

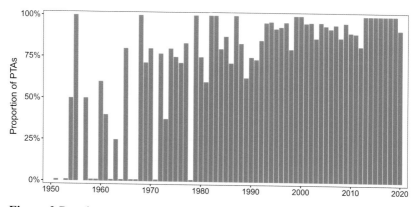

Figure 3 Bar chart, per cent of PTA with environmental provisions over time

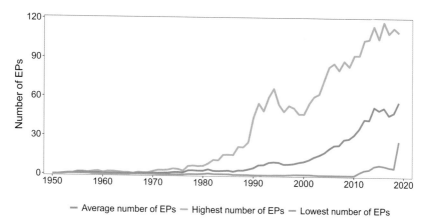

Figure 4 Number of EPs per PTA over time

provisions have only recently become more prominent in trade agreements. China is a regional leader, with an average of twenty-three environmental provisions per PTA. Yet, the Regional Comprehensive Economic Partnership (RCEP), which entered into force in 2022 between China, Australia, Japan, New Zealand, and Republic of Korea and the ten member states of the Association of Southeast Asian Nations (ASEAN) and accounts for approximately 30 per cent of global GDP, is almost silent on the environment. PTAs involving African countries have an average of twelve environmental provisions. The recently launched African Continental Free Trade Area (AfCFTA), comprising fifty-four African states, includes few environment provisions, indicating substantial untapped potential that is yet to be leveraged in future negotiations for PTAs involving African partners.

The Increasing Diversity of Environmental Provisions

Environmental provisions in PTAs are not only multiplying; they are also becoming increasingly diverse and far-reaching (see Figure 5).[11] Environmental provisions include environmental law principles, such as common but differentiated responsibilities or the polluter pays principle; provisions that regulate or refer to the level of domestic environmental protection; provisions that govern environmental law-making and policy-making, for example, demanding the participation of NGOs or citizens in the adoption of environmental measures; provisions that govern the interaction with non-environmental issues; provisions that refer to the enforcement of domestic environmental measures; provisions that encourage environmental protection; provisions that govern cooperation on environmental matters; provisions that refer to trade-related measures; provisions that focus on assistance; provisions that refer to specific environmental issues; provisions that concern the implementation of the agreements; provisions that demand the creation of new institutions; provisions that refer to the settlement of disputes; and, lastly, provisions that refer to environmental institutions, such as the Paris Agreement.

Some of these provisions entail so-called environmental exceptions that permit countries to limit trade to conserve natural resources, similar to those in the General Agreement on Tariffs and Trade (GATT) of 1947, which is now part of the WTO (GATT Article XX(b)). These exceptions are included in Figure 5 under the category 'Trade-related measures', which until recently was the most frequent type of environmental provision.

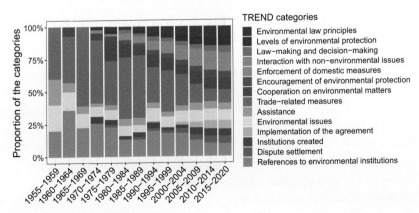

Figure 5 Types of environmental provisions

---

[11] Velut et al. (2022) offer a recent review of different approaches to environmental and social provisions in PTAs in the EU, Australia, Canada, Chile, Japan, New Zealand, Switzerland, and the US.

At the same time, PTAs have numerous environmental provisions with greater scope than the relevant provisions in the WTO. For example, some PTAs include environmental provisions that promote the harmonization, the reinforcement, and the implementation of environmental policies; back-up MEAs; demand the transfer of environmental technologies to developing countries, as well as environmental capacity-building; facilitate civil society activity; and cover manifold environmental issues, such as limiting deforestation, protecting fish stocks, reducing hazardous wastes, and mitigating CO_2 emissions. In recent years, PTAs have included an increasing number of environmental provisions that are not trade related. PTAs have become vectors for negotiating environmental obligations, which were previously debated in fora exclusively devoted to the environment.

As Figure 6 shows, the most prevalent environmental issue areas in PTAs are waste, biodiversity, water, fisheries, and forests. Environmental provisions that focus on these issues are particularly frequent in North-South and South-South PTAs. In recent years, trade agreements have increasingly addressed climate change (on the diffusion of climate-related provisions, see Section 6).

Recently, PTAs have been directly linked to many SDGs. For example, they contain provisions to encourage trade in energy-efficient goods (SDG 7), ratify the Paris Agreement (SDG 13), prevent maritime pollution (SDG 14), and protect and sustainably manage forests (SDG 15). Thus, one might expect that PTAs with environmental provisions can support the implementation of a number of SDGs and promote the environmental dimension of the 2030 Agenda for Sustainable Development. So far, the actual effects of environmental provisions in PTAs on different aspects of sustainable development have remained unclear. We will shed light on the environmental and economic consequences of environmental provisions in Section 7.

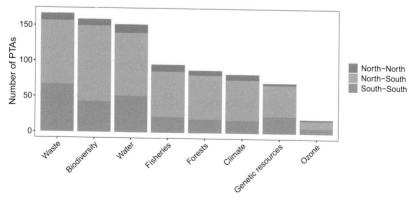

Figure 6 Number of PTAs with at least one environmental provision addressing the issue area

The Key Role of the US

The US, which has prioritized trade and environment linkages since NAFTA, raised the prominence of both labour and environmental issues in trade policy-making. Strengthening environmental standards in foreign markets to ease competitive pressure has become one of the main objectives of American trade policy. In 1992, this goal became manifest when NAFTA was adopted with a side agreement, the North American Agreement on Environmental Cooperation. One of the main aims of this side agreement was to ensure that parties would enforce their own environmental regulations. Environmental NGOs, labour unions and businesses in the US were worried that Mexico would fail to adequately enforce its domestic regulations to cut back costs and become more attractive for foreign investments (Interview with US official, 2017).

The US approach is characterized by its attention to enforcement (Velut et al., 2022). Several US agreements provide that civil society actors can file complaints for a country's failure to enforce its own environmental obligations. In some US deals, trade sanctions can be used as an enforcement tool: when there is persistent failure to enforce domestic environmental measures, an arbitral panel can levy a monetary fine, and in case of non-payment, a party has the right to trade retaliation (Morin & Rochette, 2017).[12] As a result of these mechanisms, US partners are incentivized to implement their obligations prior to the entry into force of the agreement (Bastiaens & Postnikov, 2017). This improved the implementation of measures related to the protection of endangered species in Peru, following the 2009 US-Peru PTA (Jinnah & Morin, 2020).

The Key Role of the EU

Since the 1990s, the EU has regarded itself as a normative power, actively promoting norms beyond its borders. In the context of EU trade policy, this goal has been particularly prominent since the turn of the last century (Poletti & Sicurelli, 2018). When multilateral negotiations became increasingly stuck, the EU focused on promoting PTA. The aim was to conclude comprehensive trade agreements that foster trade and investment and strengthen regulatory standards, rule of law, and sustainable development (European Commission, 2015).

---

[12] While enforcement mechanisms are strong in modern US PTAs, this was not the case in an earlier generation of agreements. In earlier generations of PTAs, enforcement mechanisms were often weak or non-existent. However, over time, the US has sought to strengthen enforcement mechanisms in its PTAs. One example in this regard was the inclusion of strong dispute settlement provisions in the United States–Mexico–Canada Agreement (USMCA), which replaced NAFTA in 2020. The USMCA includes a robust dispute settlement mechanism that allows parties to challenge each other's compliance with the agreement, with the possibility of financial penalties and retaliation.

The EU has included comprehensive Trade and Sustainable Development (TSD) chapters in its trade agreements since the 2009 PTA with South Korea. The approach in the European TSD chapters is based on three pillars: multiple environment-related commitments, many of which are linked to a range of MEAs; the participation of civil society organizations to help implement the commitments; and a dedicated dispute settlement mechanism whereby independent arbitrators make findings on compliance public (European Commission, 2018). When the UN Agenda 2030 on SDGs and the Paris Agreement were adopted in 2015, the European Commission began revising its TSD chapters. For instance, the EU-Canada Comprehensive Economic Trade Agreement, signed in 2016, includes three chapters that deal with sustainable development, labour, and the environment (Vignarelli, 2021). While the EU focuses on using trade policy and related instruments for sustainability, a review of six recent EU PTAs shows that substantial potential remains untapped, namely: the use of environmental provisions to mitigate the negative impacts of trade and the use of trade to boost environmental sustainability (Kettunen et al., 2021).

Other Players

Historically, the US and EU have played a pioneering role in extending environmental provisions, showcasing how PTAs can enable experimentation and promote innovation in the trade regime complex. However, extensive environmental provisions are now included in agreements that do not involve either party. One recent PTAs with innovative provisions in their areas of climate change was concluded in 2021 between Iceland, Liechtenstein, Norway, and the UK. It recalls the objective of limiting temperature increase to 1.5 degree above pre-industrial level, it reaffirms the parties' nationally determined contributions under the Paris Agreement, it encourages trade in goods and services that 'are of particular relevance for climate change mitigation and adaptation', it commits parties to cooperate on offshore wind generation, hydrogen technologies, and carbon capture, it supports reductions targets for international aviation and maritime transportation, and it calls for a global phase-out of fossil fuel subsides (Article 13.22).

Although environmental provisions are less frequent in PTAs between developing countries, developing and emerging economies increasingly include them in their most recent PTAs (Berger et al., 2017). Developing countries used to prioritize support for more traditional trade issues such as export competitiveness, industrialization, quality infrastructure, and trade facilitation. However, more recently, there has been a substantial increase in interest for cooperation on environmental issues, for example, by the countries of the Andean Community in their negotiations with the EU (interview with EU Commission, 15 November 2021). A growing number of developing countries are incorporating environmental provisions in South-South trade agreements (Lechner & Spilker, 2021). The trend towards linking trade and the environment in PTAs might be related to the fact that citizens in developing countries tend to support the insertion of environmental provisions in PTAs (Bernauer & Nguyen, 2015).

At the same time, some political leaders in developing countries are concerned that environmental provisions are used as a means to disguise 'green protectionism'. They argue that high-income countries try to use environmental regulations to create barriers to trade, which could limit their ability to export goods to their markets. Indeed, some negotiators are still sceptical about ambitious environmental provisions, which are promoted by high-income countries (interview with EU Commission, 24 November 2021). Developing countries are also concerned about unilateral policy approaches, such as the European CBAM.

However, leaders from developing countries are increasingly positive about linking trade and the environment in the context of preferential trade negotiations (Interview with EU Commission, 15 November 2021). Many developing countries, such as Costa Rica, are now proactively moving trade and environmental interlinkages forward in the multilateral context and in the Trade and Environmental Sustainability Structured Discussions (TESSD) recently launched at the WTO (see also Section 8). Simultaneously, developing countries favour environmental provisions related to issues that they care about deeply, such as waste, water, and biodiversity. In South-South PTAs, these issue areas are especially important (see Figure 6). For instance, Peru and Colombia have been leaders in introducing biodiversity provisions in the trade system (Morin & Gauquelin, 2016).

Governments in many developing and emerging economies seem to be moving towards a more open approach that links trade and the environment. In major emerging economies, the situation varies. As mentioned above, while China includes a substantial number of environmental provisions in its average PTA, the country has been criticized for its lack of focus on the environment in the recently concluded RCEP. In 2020, China and the EU signed a Comprehensive Agreement on Investment, which commit China to effectively implement the Paris Agreement and to make continued efforts to address climate change. India's PTAs typically include several provisions related to environmental protection, although their implementation has been criticized as insufficient. Overall, there is still significant room for improvement in major emerging economies but some progress has been made.

Compliance and Enforcement Mechanisms

Intergovernmental committees provide a framework for regular exchanges on compliance with environmental provisions. The 2011 PTA between the EU and Korea, for instance, created a Committee on Trade and Sustainable Development comprising officials from both parties. They come together regularly to discuss the implementation of environmental provisions and help define priorities for cooperation (Morin et al., 2018a).

In addition to intergovernmental mechanisms, civil society participation can help promote PTA implementation. In the EU, domestic advisory groups (DAGs), representing various branches of civil society, are set up in the EU and in each partner country to help monitor and provide advice on implementation. The establishment of civil society forums creates a space for wider civil society participation in monitoring the implementation of PTAs. Although many countries have expressed their support for the involvement of civil society in trade policymaking, a number of PTAs focus on ad hoc consultations for the implementation of PTAs instead of institutionalized civil society committees, such as EU domestic advisory groups, which meet roughly once a year (Velut et al., 2022, p. 112).

Do joint institutions created by PTAs such as intergovernmental committees or civil society forums effectively promote compliance? Insights drawn from interviews indicate that their effectiveness can be limited for several reasons (Morin et al., 2018a). Actors that are supposed to work together in the framework of these joint institutions, such as civil society actors, are not always sufficiently organized or may lack the necessary government support to make use of these options. In some joint institutions, the institutional design lacks a clear focus on environmental protection, which means that more traditional trade issues tend to overshadow environmental concerns. In other cases, the relevant institutions are never established because there is not much interest or the present institutions are considered more appropriate.

Technical assistance and capacity building also play important roles in the implementation of multiple PTAs. By now, 14 per cent of the 775 examined PTAs include provisions on technical assistance and capacity-building. In addition, 10 per cent also include financial or technology transfer commitments. For example, the US regularly offers assistance through several different measures, including training in resource management and environmental enforcement, public awareness campaigns, the transfer of environmentally friendly technologies, assistance for the creation of protected areas, and legal advice on new environmental laws (Morin et al., 2018a). Measures, such as the establishment of wastewater laboratories in Central America or the development of an electronic system for tracking timber in Peru, have been implemented. The 2006 US-Peru PTA defines US commitments for providing technologies and training for forest conservation and the protection of endangered species in Peru. As a result of the PTA, for instance, an electronic system for tracking timber has been put in place in Peru.

In some PTAs, the non-compliance with environmental provisions is subject to the PTA's dispute settlement mechanisms (DSM), which can eventually lead to trade sanctions. EU PTAs rely solely on a cooperative policy dialogue approach to enforce environmental provisions. In the event of disagreement, parties can initiate government consultations. If the dispute is not resolved during this phase, a panel of experts convenes and writes a report with recommendations to help the parties resolve the dispute. The TSD committee monitors the implementation of the panel's recommendations.[13]

Research suggests that both sanction-based and cooperative approaches can be effective (Bastiaens & Postnikov, 2017). However, the enforcement of environmental provisions remains controversial. In particular, the EU's approach to its TSD chapters is frequently criticized for being weaker (Vignarelli, 2021). Some studies find that TSD chapters (EU Commission, 2017) and environmental provisions in EU PTAs (Bastiaens & Postnikov, 2017) have been effective. However, other studies are more critical (Harrison et al., 2019). Many stakeholder groups believe that policy instruments other than trade agreements are more effective for pursuing non-trade policy goals, such as environmental protection (Yildirim et al., 2021).

In the light of this debate, the EU has recently started working on a new TSD approach to its trade agreements. In 2018, EU Trade Commissioner Cecilia Malmström unveiled a 15-Point Action Plan to increase the effectiveness of EU TSD chapters in PTAs. The plan sets out to ensure that countries comply with their commitments. It includes more assertive enforcement mechanisms, facilitates civil society's monitoring role, and makes EU resources available to support the implementation of TSD chapters. In 2021, the European Commission published its Trade Policy Review, entitled 'An Open, Sustainable and Assertive Trade Policy', which focuses on trade and sustainable development in EU PTAs. In 2021, the European Commission also initiated a review of the 15-Point Action Plan on TSD to reflect on additional steps to improve the implementation and

---

[13] New Zealand had previously opposed the general DSM applying to the environmental chapter of PTAs, but this changed during the TPP negotiations. The environmental chapter of the Comprehensive and Progressive Agreement for Trans-Pacific Partnership is subject to trade sanctions and the country may now actively seek this application in line with New Zealand's goals to encourage higher quality outcomes (Interview with New Zealand official, 2017).

enforcement of TSD chapters. Measures include 'the possibility of sanctions for noncompliance' (EU Commission, 2018).

Some scholars, experts, and civil society representatives argued that the EU should move towards the US sanction-based enforcement approach (Bronckers & Gruni, 2021).[14] Others are sceptical about the effectiveness of sanctions (Durán, 2020; Hradilova & Svoboda, 2018). For example, the recent case of the dispute between the US and Guatemala under the labour provisions of the Dominican Republic-Central America Free Trade Agreement suggests that the sanction-based approach may not be the best way to tackle non-compliance with labour and environmental standards insofar as the outcome of this dispute was a disappointment for many who had hoped for a positive precedent for workers. More generally, threats and sanctions can lead to political backlashes and counterproductive reactions. Instead, cooperation between parties and capacity-building are often regarded as more promising for promoting compliance. This is largely because some of the major obstacles to the enforcement of environmental provisions in PTAs are linked to improving civil society participation, cooperation between PTA parties, and monitoring of compliance with the PTA (Hradilova & Svoboda, 2018).

In 2022, the European Commission put forward the new communication 'The Power of Trade Partnerships: Together for Green and Just Economic Growth' on how to further strengthen the implementation and enforcement of TSD chapters in EU PTAs. For instance, in the document, the Commission proposes to strengthen provisions in new PTAs and accepts the use of trade sanctions as the recourse of last resort against instances of serious violations of these commitments. In practical terms, communication should also make it easier for Domestic Advisory Groups (DAGs) that are set up to monitor agreements to raise complaints. Although this approach still has to prove itself in practice, it seems to be a promising compromise. While a rigid sanction-based mechanism may be needed in certain contexts (Jinnah & Lindsay, 2016), it should not substitute for a softer cooperative approach (Morin et al., 2018a). Both approaches are complementary. When they exist side by side in the same trade agreement, they can induce major improvements in compliance.

The debate about the effective implementation and enforcement of environmental provisions in PTAs also concerns European trade deals under negotiation. In 2019, after two decades of negotiations, the EU and Mercosur reached a political agreement on a new trade deal that would have significant

---

[14] At the same time, according to some interviewees, labour and environmental standards in European PTAs were boosted by the panel ruling of 2021 in the EU-Korea labour dispute; other interviewees are more critical of the outcome of this ruling and the effectiveness of the cooperative EU approach

geopolitical importance for the EU. However, several EU member states, the European Parliament, and civil society organizations have strong reservations about ratifying the deal. Although the PTA includes multiple environmental provisions, environmentally concerned stakeholders are worried about its negative environmental impact and the effectiveness of its environmental provisions, especially through deforestation. In their view, the European approach to enforcement is too weak. The EU-Mercosur agreement mobilized various political interest groups, especially environmental NGOs, but also the European agricultural lobby. The deal was not ratified in 2020 as planned and was instead put on hold. The election of Brazilian President Lula in 2022 presents a fresh opportunity to revise and ultimately conclude the agreement as he is more receptive to environmental considerations than his predecessor. Overall, while the EU largely focuses on using trade policy and related instruments to achieve sustainability goals, key improvements in EU PTAs' sustainability-related provisions are required. More assertive implementation could help deliver the vision put forward by the European Green Deal, a package of policy initiatives (including climate, energy, transport, and taxation policies) to attain the EU's goal of reaching climate neutrality by 2050.

Beyond the US and EU, there is no universal approach to the enforcement of environmental content in PTAs. Enforcement varies depending on the specific agreement and countries involved. Generally, the enforcement of environmental provisions in PTAs involves a mix of mechanisms, including monitoring, dispute settlement, and cooperation. Some PTAs include all aspects, whereas others are limited to a single element. Additionally, the level of enforceability of environmental provisions differs across PTAs. They may refer to a relatively weak 'strive to ensure' approach (e.g., in earlier US agreements), a more stringent 'shall not fail to effectively enforce' approach (e.g., in recent US and New Zealand's PTAs) or an even more stringent 'shall promote compliance with and effectively enforce' environmental laws (e.g., in Canadian PTAs) (Velut et al., 2022).

Civil Society Participation

Civil society participation can improve stakeholders' input throughout the trade policy process (Velut et al., 2022, p. 20–1): First, prior to negotiations and during the negotiation phase, environmental impact assessments and civil society consultations help countries identify the problems likely to arise for compliance with the PTA. For instance, when the US-Peru FTA's Forest Annex was drafted, environmental NGOs offered substantial input. Second, during the implementation phase, technical assistance and capacity-building approaches combined with civil society participation can generate better outcomes than those that focus solely on state actors. This type of civil society engagement requires adequate funding, as in the case of the Canada-Colombia PTA in force since 2011. Third, in the context of enforcement, public submissions for non-compliance are key. For example, in 2011, a local Mexican community organization filed a submission under NAFTA's environmental side agreement, stating that the Mexican government was not adequately enforcing its environmental laws in the context of limestone extraction in the Sumidero Canyon National Park (Velut et al., 2022, p. 23). This action had a positive impact on the environment. The case of Sumidero Canyon illustrates how effective it can be to enable civil society to participate in PTA enforcement mechanisms.

Overall, environmental provisions are increasingly varied and far reaching and some can play a major role in environmental governance. However, the factors that drive the inclusion of environmental provisions in PTAs and the implications of PTA involvement in environmental governance remain unclear. Against this background, we assessed 298 different types of environmental provisions in 775 PTAs to explore why they spread (Section 4), the North-South dynamics they involve (Section 5), how they are diffused (Section 6), what effects they have (Section 7), and their potential for multilateral agreements (Section 8).

4 Drivers of Environmental Provisions in PTAs

Research on the incorporation of environmental provisions in PTAs has provided several possible explanations for what drives this trend. However, such research is typically based on case studies of individual agreements, such as NAFTA and its side agreement on environmental cooperation. Although NAFTA offers significant insights, the drivers that apply to this specific agreement may not necessarily apply to the broader set of existing PTAs. As we approach the three-decade mark since the implementation of NAFTA, and with hundreds of PTAs now featuring increasingly diverse and extensive environmental content, it is imperative that we expand our focus beyond single-case analysis.

To date, systematic research on the various drivers of environmental provisions across the entire universe of trade agreements remains limited primarily because of the lack of comprehensive data on the environmental content of PTAs. This section discusses existing scholarship on various drivers of environmental provisions and analyses why particular types of countries may prefer specific types of environmental provisions. Through this approach, we hope to deepen our understanding of the drivers of environmental provisions in PTAs.

Box 1 Sustainable palm oil in the Comprehensive Economic Partnership Agreement (CEPA): A new mechanism to strengthen environmental protection through trade

In 2018, Indonesia signed the Comprehensive Economic Partnership Agreement (CEPA) with the European Free Trade Association, which includes Iceland, Lichtenstein, Norway, and Switzerland. The CEPA went into effect in 2021 and includes an innovative regulatory mechanism designed to encourage environmental protection through international trade. Specifically, for palm oil imports, the tariff reductions under CEPA only apply to Indonesian palm oil that meets specific sustainability criteria, such as ending deforestation, peat drainage, and fire clearing (Sieber-Gasser, 2021). Swiss importers of Indonesian palm oil must ensure that their imports are certified under the voluntary sustainability standard of the Roundtable on Sustainable Palm Oil (RSPO) to benefit from CEPA tariff preferences.

Although Switzerland only imports small amounts of Indonesian palm oil, the environmental provision under CEPA could serve as a precedent for future PTAs. This is especially relevant to the ongoing negotiations between the EU and Indonesia for a PTA, where palm oil trade remains a contentious issue (Brock, 2022). Indonesia has proposed certifying 'sustainability' under the Indonesian Sustainable Palm Oil (ISPO) scheme, but the EU is unlikely to accept it due to its perceived shortcomings. Nevertheless, the new regulatory mechanism under CEPA has the potential to promote sustainability through trade beyond the palm oil sector.

Response to Electoral Pressures or a Sceptical Public

The inclusion of environmental provisions in PTAs might be driven by the hope of making these PTAs more palatable to a sceptical public (Bastiaens & Postnikov, 2020), including pro-environmental political parties and non-state actors opposed to trade liberalization, who would otherwise prevent the conclusion of trade agreements (Gallagher, 2004; Hufbauer et al., 2000). For instance, American environmental NGOs put pressure on the US government in 1992 to incorporate environmental provisions in NAFTA (Gallagher, 2004).

The view that environmental provisions are a response to these types of pressure is supported by the fact that democracies incorporate more environmental provisions in their trade agreements than autocracies (Morin et al., 2018b). Democracies (Polity2 score greater than 16) contain on average six times more environmental provisions than autocracies. Figure 7 shows the correlation between the Polity2 score (Marshall et al., 2020) of a country and

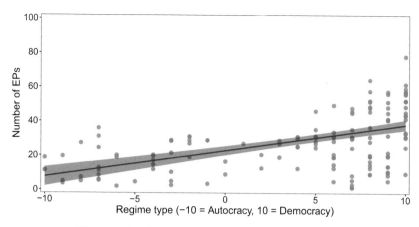

Figure 7 Regime type and environmental provision

the average number of provisions in PTAs concluded between 2000 and 2020. At the same time, some PTAs with democratic members have few environmental provisions.

Environmental Objectives

A second driver is that policymakers make use of PTAs to improve environmental regulations, and that PTAs' environmental provisions are used to push environmental objectives beyond typical environmental institutions (Jinnah & Lindsay, 2016; Johnson, 2015). Negotiations in multilateral environmental fora advance slowly. By contrast, trade negotiations between a smaller set of countries can facilitate the inclusion of extensive environmental obligations by enabling trade-offs across different issue areas and by side-stepping countries that block progress. This is in line with a survey in which negotiators stated that they use PTAs' environmental provisions to promote environmental protection (George, 2014).

Both the US and the EU use environmental provisions to spread their domestic norms across the world (Jinnah and Lindsay, 2016; Poletti and Sicurelli, 2016). For instance, the US can extract more commitments on forestry and endangered species when these issues are negotiated in the context of a trade agreement (Jinnah, 2011). In fact, some provisions on endangered species in the 2009 US-Peru PTA are more detailed and characterized by better enforceability than those included in the Convention on International Trade in Endangered Species of Wild Fauna and Flora (CITES). These environmental provisions 'have the potential to enhance environmental regime effectiveness in ways that have been impossible under environmental treaties alone' (Jinnah, 2011, p. 191).

In the EU, trade agreements are frequently used to promote non-trade goals, including environmental protection. The aim is to use trade as leverage to promote environmental standards (interview with EU Commission, 24 November 2021). In particular, the EU has gradually integrated its climate agenda into its trade negotiations. As early as 1979, the Lomé II Convention, concluded between Europe and African, Caribbean and Pacific countries, promoted renewable energy and energy efficiency. In 1989, before the first report of the Intergovernmental Panel on Climate Change was published, the Lomé Convention was revised to include a reference to the greenhouse effect. In the 1990s, certain EU trade agreements reaffirmed the importance of international cooperation on climate change and incorporated increasingly detailed provisions. Today, climate change provisions are part of all recent EU trade agreements. Climate change has gradually become a key element in EU trade negotiations, directly contributing to EU environmental objectives.

Interest in the use of trade agreements to promote environmental objectives is in line with the observation that greener countries tend to include more environmental provisions in their trade agreements. As shown in Figure 8, a higher Environmental Protection Index (EPI) correlates with a greater number of environmental provisions.[15] An increase of the EPI by ten points is associated with four additional environmental provisions in PTAs. Environmental leaders incorporate more environmental provisions in their PTAs than laggards.

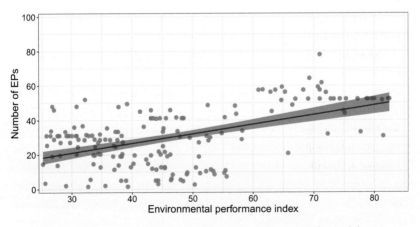

Figure 8 Environmental protection and environmental provisions

---

[15] This pattern could also be shaped by the fact that a country with stricter domestic environmental regulations faces lower compliance costs for domestic constituencies (Downs et al., 1996; Milewicz et al., 2018; Sprinz and Vaahtoranta, 1994) and, thus, has less to lose when its regulations are diffused across the world.

Safeguard against Trade Disputes

Another explanation is that negotiators include environmental provisions in PTAs in response to trade disputes (Pauwelyn, 2014), which frequently concern domestic environmental regulations. Some of the most well-known GATT/WTO disputes are related to environmental standards, including the tuna-dolphin and the shrimp-turtle (see Box 2). In fact, a number of environmental provisions help preserve countries' regulatory sovereignty in favour of environmental protection, while shielding countries against legal disputes of this type. We refer to these as defensive environmental provisions. They safeguard a country's policy space for environmental regulations and prevent countries from being involved in legal disputes (Blümer et al., 2020). A widespread example of a defensive environmental provision is the exception to trade commitments for domestic measures deemed necessary to protect the life of plants and animals (GATT Article XX(b)).

BOX 2 ENVIRONMENTAL DISPUTES IN THE GATT/WTO

The General Agreement on Tariffs and Trade (GATT) and its successor, the WTO, have been the centre of many environmental disputes since their creation. While their primary objective is to facilitate international trade and reduce trade barriers, environmental concerns often conflict with these goals.

One of the most significant environmental disputes in the GATT/WTO concerns the US ban on tuna imports. In 1991, the US enacted a law that required all tuna caught using a fishing method that harmed dolphins to be labelled as 'dolphin-safe' and banned from importation. Mexico, which relied heavily on this fishing method, challenged the law at the GATT.

Another landmark dispute in the WTO was the shrimp turtle case, which arose in the late 1990s between the US and several Asian countries including India, Malaysia, Pakistan, and Thailand. The case centred on a US law that required shrimp imports to be caught using methods that did not harm sea turtles. The affected countries argued that the law violated the principles of the GATT/WTO by discriminating against their shrimp exports. Although the case was ultimately settled in 2001, with the WTO ruling in favour of the US, it led to significant changes in the way that environmental concerns are addressed within the WTO. This includes the creation of a committee on trade and environment and the recognition of the importance of sustainable development in trade policy. The shrimp turtle case remains a significant example of the tension between trade and environmental protection in the WTO and highlights the need for a balance between the two.

It is noteworthy that countries that most often part of trade disputes also tend to have the highest number of environmental provisions in their trade agreements (Morin et al., 2017). The US, the EU, and Canada are most commonly involved in disputes that concern environmental measures, whether in the multilateral setting or within the context of regional dispute settlement mechanisms. They also belong to the most innovative countries in terms of environmental provisions in PTAs. The tuna-dolphin case was still very contentious and drove the mobilization of environmental NGOs in the US, when President Bill Clinton declared that he would refuse to sign the NAFTA implementing bill, unless it contained a side agreement on the environment.

Investor-state disputes can also be a contributing factor. Several disputes opposing a foreign investor to a host state concern environmental regulations. They include the Metalclad, Ethyl, Myers, Methanex, Lone Pine, and Vattenfall cases. In response, environmental provisions were incorporated into the investment chapter of recent PTAs, including a recognition of the parties' right to exercise discretion with respect to environmental matters and a clarification that non-discriminatory regulatory actions designed to protect the environment do not constitute indirect expropriation (Gagné & Morin, 2006).

It appears that even cases before the European Court of Justice can lead to new environmental provisions (Morin et al., 2017, p. 382). A dispute between Austria and the European Commission is a compelling case. In order to maintain the quality of the air, Austria passed regulations in 2003 prohibiting lorries exceeding 7.5 tons and carrying specific items from using a part of the A12 freeway. In 2005, the European Court of Justice equated the measure to a quantitative restriction to trade, which could not be justified on environmental grounds because the objective could be attained with less restrictive measures. Some months down the road, the 2006 Albania–EU Stabilization and Association Agreement contained a first-time provision stating that 'exceptional national standards [on gaseous and particulate emissions for heavy goods vehicles] should be avoided' and 'vehicles which comply with [international environmental standards] may operate without further restriction in the territory of the parties' (Protocol 5, Article 15).

Green Protectionism

Environmental provisions may also be used in response to protectionist pressure from interest groups, including import-competing companies and business lobbies (Dür et al., 2022). Environmental provisions can limit trade in several ways. For instance, provisions that demand more stringent environmental regulations abroad reduce competition from foreign firms. When they limit trade in particular items, such as chemical products or dangerous waste, environmental provisions in PTAs may have a more overt protectionist effect. Therefore, environmental provisions may actually be window-dressing to conceal protectionist goals (Bechtel et al., 2012; Bhagwati & Hudec, 1996; Krugman, 1997; Lechner, 2016).

The hypothesis that protectionism drives the inclusion of certain environmental provisions is supported by the observation that trade agreements with large distributional effects tend to include more environmental provisions (Morin et al., 2018b). When a high-income country negotiates a trade agreement with a large developing country, the former often insists on the inclusion of environmental provisions as a necessary condition to level the playing field for its domestic industries. In contrast, trade negotiators in developing countries often condemn these provisions for being no more than sophisticated non-tariff barriers to trade.

While some companies might favour stricter environmental provisions in PTAs to ease competition from abroad, firms might also have an interest in environmental provisions to expand their business. They might see in environmental provision an opportunity to alter the domestic competitive landscape in a manner that benefits them. In addition, firms might favour broader and more stringent environmental provisions to harmonize regulations across countries, thereby reducing transaction costs for their transnational business activities. However, it is difficult to find evidence that businesses actively promote environmental provisions in PTAs. Very few environmental provisions in PTAs provide the basis for regulatory harmonization, which would reduce transaction costs. Instead, companies frequently discourage governments from implementing environmental regulations as they might increase operational and compliance costs. Overall, existing research suggests that the role of the private sector as a driver of environmental provisions in PTA varies across countries and sectors (Lechner, 2018). For example, while companies involved in the production of environmental goods are likely to favour and lobby for their diffusion, firms in polluting sectors are unlikely to do so (see also Brandi et al., 2020).

Duplication and Diffusion

Finally, environmental provisions may simply spread due to duplication (Allee & Elsig, 2016), policy diffusion (Elkins & Simmons, 2005), and network effects. Because of these dynamics, a newly inserted environmental provision can diffuse rapidly in the trade regime complex and cause an increase in the number of provisions found in each subsequent agreement (Milewicz et al., 2018).

At least four factors contribute to the diffusion process. First, countries may seek to duplicate the most stringent clauses from their earlier PTAs to level the playing field and ensure that similar regulatory conditions are imposed on their trade competitors. Second, negotiators may draw inspiration from PTAs involving the most powerful countries because they want to demonstrate their regulatory alignment and raise their profile as candidates for future PTAs. Third, they may attempt to reduce transaction costs in the negotiation and implementation stages by simply duplicating the most common clauses in the trade system. Fourth, they may choose to include environmental clauses considered to be the most effective from a trade or environmental standpoint by drawing on the experience of earlier PTAs.

For example, several countries that have signed a PTA with the EU now include climate-related provisions in their own PTAs with third parties. Consequently, the EU is part to a declining share of trade agreements that deal with climate change. In 1995, the EU was party to more than 70 per cent of agreements that included a provision related to climate change. In 2020, only 34 per cent of agreements that contain at least one provision on climate change are EU agreements.

Drivers across Different Provisions

To better understand what drives the adoption of environmental provisions in PTAs, we investigated why certain countries prefer certain types of environmental provisions (Blümer et al., 2020). We distinguished between defensive and offensive environmental provisions. As mentioned above, defensive provisions safeguard a country's policy space for environmental regulation. A well-known example of a defensive environmental provision is the exception to trade commitments for domestic measures necessary to protect human, animal, and plant life and health. Another example of a defensive provision is the precautionary principle, which protects parties' right to regulate, even when there is a lack of scientific certainty over the negative externalities of the regulated subject matter. By contrast, offensive provisions demand the introduction and enforcement of specific environmental policies. Examples include commitments to implement a list of environmental agreements, reduce subsidies to fisheries, adopt specific emissions standards for vehicles, and promote environmental protection in various issue areas. Consider, for instance, the 2000 US-Jordan PTA with its provisions on the protection of 'fragile coral reef ecosystems in the Gulf of Aqaba'.

Overall, our data analysis shows that negotiators tend to embrace defensive environmental provisions that safeguard a country's policy space in their trade agreements (Blümer et al., 2020). This substantiates the view that environmental provisions are partly driven by trade disputes, because they aim to safeguard countries' policy space for domestic regulations geared toward environmental protection. This general tendency to adopt defensive provisions indicates that countries prefer to modify their environmental regulations freely, in line with their own policy objectives. These provisions can be seen as a means of protecting democratic processes.

The growth in the number of defensive provisions also reflects the increasing depth of PTAs (Dür et al., 2014). Recent PTAs include a range of trade issues that is constantly expanding, and commonly include issues such as intellectual property, services, public procurement, and agriculture. Because each of these new chapters includes new trade commitments, states agree on new defensive environmental exceptions to limit these commitments.

Since the early 2000s, the average number of offensive provisions per PTA has grown more rapidly than the number of defensive provisions. In particular, countries with strict environmental regulations and strong bargaining power tend to favour offensive provisions that require the introduction of specific environmental policies.[16] This indicates that they are using PTAs to push forward and strengthen environmental objectives worldwide. Moreover, by levelling the playing field, they reduce the trade pressure from countries with weaker regulations. For example, the EU uses its 'trade power to achieve non-trade objectives' (Meunier & Nicolaïdis, 2006, p. 912). In North America, 'large asymmetry in power among countries proved to be crucial for the US's ability to reopen [NAFTA] negotiations and secure side agreements' (Aggarwal, 2013, p. 102). For the US, as mentioned in Section 3, a major reason for incorporating environmental provisions in PTAs is to promote a level-playing field. Given their strong bargaining power, the EU and the US have been able to insert many offensive provisions in their trade agreements.

Over time, a trend has emerged with increasingly 'offensive' environmental provisions in trade agreements, which demand the introduction of particular environmental policies and warrant their enforcement. The share of offensive environmental provisions has increased slightly in the last twenty-five years (Figure 9). In absolute numbers, the growth is striking. While the average PTA included fewer than four offensive provisions in the early 1990s, the average PTAs included more than eighteen offensive provisions in the 2016–2020 period. Trade negotiators are increasingly using environmental provisions in trade agreements as a means to leverage environmental objectives worldwide. Rather than treating environmental protection as merely an exception to trade commitments, an increasing number of states are using PTAs as

---

[16] While high-income countries might impose green agendas, they may also lag behind in terms of environmental provisions in trade agreements.

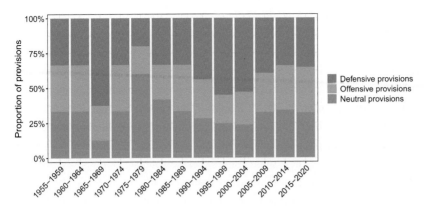

Figure 9 Defensive and offensive environmental provisions in PTAs

instruments for diffusing their environmental standards to other countries (Cima, 2018; Morin and Rochette, 2017; Poletti and Sicurelli, 2016).

As mentioned in Section 2, environmental provisions in PTAs can be characterized as 'catalytic' interlinkages (Betsill et al., 2015) insofar as they are designed to facilitate action. A prime example of such 'catalytic' interlinkages can be seen in US PTAs, which feature environmental provisions demanding stronger compliance with MEAs (Jinnah & Morin, 2020). However, our analysis of a wide range of existing PTAs indicates that numerous non-US trade agreements also strive to catalyse action, for instance, by encouraging trading partners to adopt more stringent environmental regulations. This trend is evident in the TREND data, which reveals an increasing number of offensive provisions in PTAs that amount to 'catalytic' trade and environment interlinkages by catalysing action through calls for stricter environmental regulations (Figure 9).

Environmental provisions in US PTAs that demand stronger compliance with MEAs are a good illustration of catalytic interlinkages (Jinnah & Morin, 2020). At the same time, several non-US trade agreements seek to catalyse action as well, for instance, by asking trading partners to adopt more stringent environmental regulations. In fact, as the TREND data on offensive provisions show (Figure 9), environmental provisions in trade agreements increasingly seek to catalyse action by asking trading partners to adopt more stringent environmental regulations.

Offensive environmental provisions remain insufficient (Blümer et al., 2020). The rising number of offensive provisions has been shaped by patterns of trade negotiations since the 1990s. Earlier trade agreements were intra-regional and were adopted by countries with comparable levels of environmental regulations. More recent PTAs, on the other hand, tend to be cross-regional and bring together heterogeneous countries, which increases political opportunities for levelling the regulatory playing field. However, if offensive provisions are to raise environmental standards in all participating countries and not only level the playing field, environmental provisions must be incorporated in PTAs involving countries with equally high standards.

To sum up, we have identified multiple drivers that promote the inclusion of environmental provisions in PTAs, including responding to electoral pressures for greater environmental protection, better safeguarding against environmental trade disputes, and promoting environmental governance in the context of trade negotiations. Our research also highlights the importance of power and regulatory asymmetries in driving the adoption of certain types of environmental provisions, particularly offensive provisions. This helps explain why some PTAs contain strong and enforceable provisions related to biodiversity conservation and deforestation, as high-income countries may view many developing countries as not adequately addressing these issues. In contrast, trade agreements may be vague and unassertive on sensitive topics such as climate change. This raises important questions about the negotiation dynamics between high-income and developing countries in the context of PTAs.

To further explore these dynamics, the next section delves into the interplay between trade and environmental governance in North-South negotiations.

5 North-South Dynamics

One of the key impediments to tackling environmental challenges is the alleged trade-off between economic growth and greening the economy. Some studies show that both goals can be pursued simultaneously (Prakash & Potoski, 2017). However, there are many sceptics, especially in poorer countries. Developing countries often sign trade agreements to enhance trade flows. They are concerned that the inclusion of non-trade issues, such as environmental provisions, could be used for 'green protectionism' and undermine their economic interests (Draper et al., 2017). By contrast, high-income countries, which generally have higher domestic environmental standards, tend to promote their own environmental standards in their trade agreements with developing countries.

Drawing on our data on environmental provisions in PTAs, we find that the higher the per capita income in a country, the greener the country's PTAs tend to be (Figure 10). Several PTAs between developing countries include only a few modest environmental provisions. Examples include the 2017 China–Georgia Agreement and the 2019 Agreement between Bosnia and Herzegovina and Turkey. Other South-South agreements are more ambitious, such as the 2020 Agreement between China and Ecuador. From an environmental perspective,

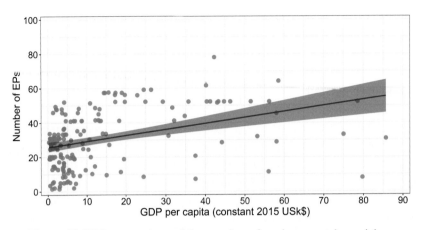

Figure 10 GDP per capita and the number of environmental provisions

the fact that these countries strive to leverage environmental protection world-wide is positive. However, concerns about 'green protectionism' in the context of North/South agreements remain particularly acute in developing countries. In Section 7, we examine questions regarding the economic effects of environmental provisions. In this section, we look more closely at how PTAs are negotiated between different types of country groups, particularly high-income and developing countries.

Trade and Aid Interlinkages

We explore the bargaining process that drives the inclusion of environmental provisions in North-South PTAs by carefully examining aid commitments. Development aid acts as a side payment in several policy fields (Baccini & Urpelainen, 2012). Therefore, one way to make environmental provisions more acceptable is to provide more aid. This could benefit donors backing PTAs with environmental provisions as well as recipient countries seeking financial assistance.

The existence of interlinkages between trade negotiations and development assistance is hardly surprising, given the high level of coordination between relevant policy actors. For instance, the US Trade Representative emphasizes the significance of linking trade and development (Government Accountability Office, 2005; see also Congress Research Service, 2008). In the EU, consultations frequently involve different Directorate Generals (DGs) of the EU Commission (interview with EU Commission, 15 November 2021; interview with EU Commission, 24 November 2021). The EU and its member countries are committed to policy coherence for development to ensure that various policy-making processes (including trade policy) consider development effects (see also Bondi and Hoekman, 2022).

Aid as a Side Payment?

The findings of our recent quantitative analysis show a positive association between the number of environmental provisions in North-South PTAs and bilateral aid commitments during PTA negotiations (Brandi et al., 2022). This positive link is particularly prominent just before the PTA is signed. It is also strongly driven by the two largest donors, the EU and the US. These two entities usually use PTA templates and offer developing countries a limited say on the content of trade agreements (e.g., Allee & Elsig, 2019; Peacock et al., 2019). This indicates that aid is used as a side payment to seal the deal and agree on previously prepared treaty content. The more environmental provisions there are in the template, the more development assistance is committed to facilitate the signature of the PTA.

The empirical evidence provided by our quantitative analysis is consistent with insights gathered during interviews. For instance, the US government regards aid as an instrument to raise the likelihood 'to complete negotiations' (Congress Research Service, 2008, p. 26). In the context of the Central America Free Trade Agreement (CAFTA) between the US and several Central American countries, a 'USTDA official said that the process of providing aid] had helped negotiators "sell" CAFTA to CAFTA countries' (Government Accountability Office, 2005, p. 28). In the EU, according to an official at the EU Commission, aid is also used as a carrot to promote trade negotiations. The EU frequently has to 'pay' if it wants to incorporate far-reaching TSD chapters in its PTAs, including by providing development assistance (interview with EU Commission, 24 November 2021).[17]

Upon closer analysis, the positive link between environmental provisions and development aid is more pronounced in the case of defensive provisions. The latter offer policy space for environmental regulation and include environmental exceptions, which allow countries to limit trade for environmental purposes. Defensive provisions are particularly appealing to high-income countries because they can use regulations, subsidies and other measures to safeguard their domestic industries. By contrast, existing trade rules strongly restrict their leeway to use tariffs. Developing countries, however, can use tariffs with more flexible because of the special and differential treatment principles that exist in

---

[17] When the EU negotiates with large emerging economies, the focus tends to be on concessions for market access in exchange for the inclusion of TSD chapters (interview with German government, September 2021).

the global trading system. Thus, developing countries are far less likely to use other forms of protectionism. In addition, they are often dubious about what motivates high-income countries to push defensive provisions, because defensive measures can restrict their access to high-income countries' markets.

The positive relationship between PTAs with environmental provisions and aid is more pronounced in recipient countries with relatively weak environmental performance (Brandi et al., 2022). At the same time, for these developing countries, the number of environmental provisions in PTAs is positively associated with development aid. This association can be observed before and after the signature of new PTAs. This finding indicates that development assistance has the potential for promoting the shift towards sustainability in these countries – a mechanism that formerly went unnoticed. Notwithstanding the controversies about whether development aid is effective for fostering growth, our findings suggest that development aid can partly explain the diffusion of environmental provisions. Recent research finds that aid for environmental projects is positively related with trade in environment-intensive goods (Hoekman et al., 2023). Coming back to the theoretical framework introduced in Section 2, this suggests that development aid, by promoting trade and environmental interlinkages, may reinforce the synergies between trade and environmental policy (see also Section 7).

Developing Countries Shaping Environmental Provisions

Some developing countries support the idea of including environmental provisions in PTAs irrespective of the provision of foreign aid. Figure 11 shows that, on average, some developing countries have a relatively high number of environmental provisions in their PTAs. Examples include Chile, Vietnam,

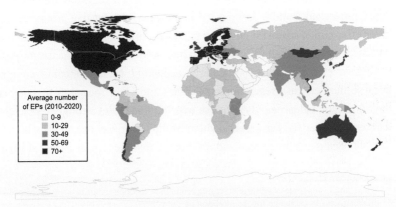

Figure 11 Average number of environmental provisions by country

Nicaragua, and Georgia. This trend is not driven solely by asymmetrical North-South agreements.

Several South-South agreements also include environmental provisions, especially for environmental issues that are a priority for them. Recent research finds that environmental provisions in South-South PTAs are not simply a by-product of a diffusion process from North-South agreements. Instead, empirical evidence indicates that environmental provisions in South-South PTAs signal a genuine commitment to environmental performance (Lechner & Spilker, 2021). As we will set out in more detail in Section 8, this is in line with previous research that shows that environmental provisions in South-South PTAs are associated with higher environmental performance (Zhou et al., 2017) and more environmental legislation (Brandi et al., 2019). These findings suggest that decision-makers can take some encouragement from the fact that trade negotiators in the Global South often commit to protecting the environment in their trade agreements without being compelled to do so by the Global North.

In some cases, developing countries have successfully extracted concessions in their negotiations with high-income countries. The agreement between Peru and the US is a case in point. One of Peru's environmental priorities is to protect genetic resources (Morin & Gauquelin, 2016). Several of its PTAs include provisions that govern access to genetic resources and sharing the benefits derived from their use. Peru is rich in biodiversity and uses trade negotiations as levers for obligations set out in the *Convention on Biological Diversity* and the *Nagoya Protocol on Genetic Resources*. These obligations concern the protection of traditional ecological knowledge, the requirement to obtain prior informed consent before accessing genetic material, and the transfer of monetary and technological benefits to genetic resource providers. For example, the 2006 US-Peru agreement includes a provision stating that the parties 'recognize the importance of respecting and preserving traditional knowledge and practices of indigenous and other communities that contribute to the conservation and sustainable use of biological diversity' (18.01.03). In a side agreement, the parties also acknowledge the importance of obtaining informed consent before gaining access to genetic resources and of sharing the benefits derived from the use of traditional knowledge and genetic resources. Moreover, the side agreement tacitly acknowledges the risk of misappropriation of genetic resources by accentuating the significant role of the quality of patent applications to safeguard that the conditions of patentability are fulfilled. In the light of the notorious US refusal to ratify the Convention on Biological Diversity, the insertion of such provisions in a US PTA is noteworthy (see also Morin & Rochette, 2017). This is a further example showing that foreign countries can influence environmental provisions in US trade agreements.

The insights provided above regarding the drivers of environmental provision and North-South dynamics in the context of trade agreements raise important questions about the potential environmental and economic impacts of including environmental provisions in trade agreements, particularly for developing countries. Therefore, there is a need to further explore the effects of environmental provisions in trade agreements and determine whether they are advantageous or disadvantageous to developing countries.

In the upcoming section, we will focus on examining the general diffusion patterns and consequences of environmental provisions in PTAs. Additionally, we will explore the specific implications of these provisions for developing countries. Through this analysis, we aim to provide a comprehensive understanding of the potential benefits and drawbacks of incorporating environmental provisions into trade agreements.

6 The Diffusion of Environmental Provisions in PTAs

When negotiating new trade agreements, trade negotiators often adopt existing environmental provisions from other PTAs. This practice of copying policy models from one polity to another is known as policy diffusion (Elkins and Simmons, 2005, pp. 34–5; Blatter et al., 2022). For example, the 2018 Comprehensive and Progressive Agreement for Trans-Pacific Partnership (CPTTP), which includes a record 137 environmental provisions, copied all of them from former PTAs with the exception of a novel provision on fisheries. In this section, we explore the spread of environmental provisions in PTAs and examine the conditions for their successful diffusion. We analyse the factors that facilitate or hinder the diffusion of environmental provisions across different PTAs, drawing on examples from diverse countries. Our focus is on understanding how policy diffusion can contribute to the dissemination of environmental best practices in international trade. Through this analysis, we aim to provide insights that can inform trade negotiations and enhance the effectiveness of environmental provisions in PTAs.

Policy Diffusion and Environmental Provisions

Let us consider the example of the diffusion of a provision, which states that specific MEAs should take priority over the PTA in the event of a legal conflict. This environmental provision was inserted into the trade system for the first time, when NAFTA was concluded in 1992. Since then, it has been successively duplicated in multiple PTAs, including in trade agreements that do not include any NAFTA countries, such as the 2008 PTA between the Association of Southeast Asian Nations and Japan.

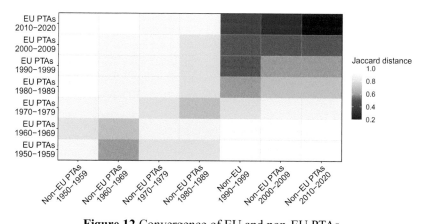

Figure 12 Convergence of EU and non-EU PTAs

Certain environmental provisions have been replicated in over 100 trade agreements, whereas others are seldom incorporated into subsequent PTAs or remain unique (Morin and Gauthier-Nadeau, 2017). For instance, the provision that demands the ratification of the Montreal Protocol on the Ozone Layer only appears once in the 1993 PTA founding the Common Market for Eastern and Southern Africa (COMESA). This raises the question: Why are some environmental provisions diffused more successfully than others? This section investigates how environmental provisions spread beyond their original PTA, and why certain environmental provisions are diffused more than others.

A closer look at trade agreements involving major trading powers shows how PTAs evolve over time. It also reveals a pattern of convergence: EU PTAs and non-EU PTAs have become more similar over time, as shown in Figure 12 (see also Morin and Rochette, 2017). In the figure, European PTAs can be found on the y-axis and non-EU PTAs on the x-axis, chronologically ordered. In the light of the Jaccard distance measures, older EU PTAs are quite different from non-EU PTAs, as shown by the pale yellow boxes. In contrast, the environmental provisions included in more recent EU-PTAs are more similar to non-EU deals, as shown by the lower distance measures in orange and red. This suggests that there is a degree of convergence between EU and non-EU agreements. EU and non-EU negotiators have learned and borrowed from each other over time, and their PTAs have become more similar as a result.

Network analysis illustrates that the EU has been a major driver of incorporating non-trade provisions since its early stages (Milewicz et al., 2018). By 1989, the EU had already established an extensive PTA network with nineteen other states, mostly located nearby, fourteen of which included environmental provisions. The EU's PTA network grew rapidly, reaching twenty-nine partners by

1999. While the EU has been linking trade and environmental issues in PTAs for a considerable amount of time, the US began doing so only in the 1990s. It was not until 2004 that the US witnessed a significant rise in the number of PTAs, and remarkably, all of them included a high number of environmental provisions. This trend has continued, and a few of the US's partners, such as Peru and Chile, have also established PTAs with environmental provisions among themselves, indicating the US's vital role in this diffusion (Milewicz et al., 2018).

To illustrate how specific types of environmental provisions spread throughout the world, let us consider a network analysis of climate provisions (see Morin and Jinnah, 2018 for an earlier version). Figure 13 shows how the network of PTAs with climate provisions has evolved over time. Each node represents a PTA member, and each tie indicates that they are connected by an agreement with at least one climate provision. As the figure illustrates, the EU is the most central actor in the network (for further information about the EU as climate norms leader in PTAs, see also Dent, 2021 and Benson et al., 2022).

However, the EU is still struggling to diffuse its approach beyond its direct trading partners. More generally, thirty-seven countries have failed to address climate change in their trade agreements, and major greenhouse gas emitters such as the US, India, and China have very few weak provisions in their PTAs. The US has incorporated some climate-related issues in its more recent agreements, including on renewable energy and energy efficiency. Nevertheless, PTAs remain underutilized instruments for promoting climate action. We have yet to explore the following: how PTAs could help disarm 'climate-negative' multilateral trade rules, which currently limit the use of climate mitigation measures because of their potential impact on trade (such as carbon border adjustments); and how PTAs could promote 'climate-positive' measures (such as fossil fuel subsidy prohibitions). On both counts, PTAs can promote the advancement of climate goals.

Explaining Diffusion Is Important

To improve our understanding of the determinants of the spread of environmental provisions and contribute to the literature on policy diffusion, we analysed the diffusion rates of environmental provisions in PTAs (Morin et al., 2019a). Explaining the diffusion rates of PTA environmental provisions is important for several reasons. First, as mentioned above, diffusion significantly influences the trade and environment interplay in the context of trade agreements because negotiators often copy environmental provisions that have been included in previous PTAs (Allee & Elsig, 2016).

Figure 13 Diffusion of climate-related provisions

Second, several studies suggest that the inclusion of environment-related content in PTAs is linked to better environmental protection (see Section 7). Therefore, understanding the conditions for their spread matters for people who care about environmental protection.

Third, studying the diffusion of environmental provisions is important in the light of the theoretical frameworks introduced in Section 2. A better understanding of the diffusion of environmental provisions sheds light on the forces that prevent the increasingly fragmented trade regime complex from stumbling into a regulatory chaos. In other words, it helps us to understand the factors that glue the complex together by encouraging policy convergence via diffusion.

Fourth, studying when environmental provisions spread is essential because it provides insights into their potential multilateralization (see also Section 8). If powerful countries alone push the multilateralization of environmental provisions, it would be regarded as a hegemonic undertaking. If driven by environmental leaders, it may be perceived more positively. Countries that can be regarded as environmental leaders but not economic superpowers include New Zealand, Bahamas, Costa Rica, and Botswana.[18]

Determinants of Diffusion: Power or Credibility?

Do the initial conditions that prevail when provisions first emerge in the trade system determine the scope of their diffusion? Which initial conditions enable a successful policy diffusion? Most of the literature on policy diffusion attempts to explain the diffusion process and examine different causal mechanisms, which can be grouped into four main categories: coercion, competition, learning, and emulation (Blatter et al., 2022; Elkins & Simmons, 2005). 'Learning' refers to a cognitive process that relies on the success of policies; 'competition' refers to processes in which countries adjust their policies because they compete with other countries; 'coercion' occurs when powerful states drive less powerful ones into adopt specific policies; and 'emulation' refers to processes in which actors are steered by principles of appropriateness (Gilardi & Wasserfallen, 2019).

Rather than looking at these diffusion processes directly, we focus on identifying factors related to the conditions of emergence that trigger successful diffusion processes. Based on our empirical findings, we can then reflect on these conditions of emergence are related to different causal mechanisms behind diffusion processes. In particular, we shed light on the processes of 'coercion' and 'learning'. While 'learning' is assumed to take place in symmetric constellations, 'coercion' is typically assumed to occur in an asymmetric setup (Blatter et al., 2022). The latter is relevant for PTAs because many of them are characterized by a high level of power asymmetries.

Based on our large-n analysis, we find that on average, provisions introduced in the framework of intercontinental agreements, which typically have more diverse country partners, diffuse more than others (Morin et al., 2019a). This finding supports the idea that 'learning' plays a key role. The policy diffusion

---

[18] These examples are selected on the basis of the 2022 Environmental Performance Index (EPI), which provides a quantitative basis for comparing environmental performance for 180 countries. New Zealand and Bahamas are both in the Top 30 while Botswana is the top-scoring African country ranked as number 35 worldwide. In fact, New Zealand is a frontrunner at the trade-environment interface. In 2019, it initiated the Agreement on Climate Change, Trade and Sustainability (ACCTS) together with Costa Rica, Fiji, Iceland, and Norway, to promote trade policies that support climate and environmental objectives.

literature finds that countries learn from cultural reference groups (Simmons & Elkins, 2004) and frequently adopt policies from countries in their region (Simmons et al., 2008; Weyland, 2005). Within the region, exchanges among trade officials and other decision-makers, as well as NGOs and the private sector across their various networks, offer multiple possibilities for dialogue and learning about the design of PTAs. Because of these mechanisms of learning and socialization, if, for instance, a Central American country includes specific environmental provisions, other countries in the region might then decide that these provisions are acceptable or even useful in the light of their own needs and capacities. Since countries tend to be open to signing an agreement if their neighbouring countries have previously concluded a similar PTA, the adoption of certain environmental provisions in intercontinental agreements sends a strong signal to others in the regions concerned, opening up new opportunities for policy learning (Poulsen, 2014). Furthermore, when countries from different regions agree to include a new environmental provision in cross-regional PTAs, the provision is more likely to be relevant to and accepted by many other countries. Therefore, a novel provision first introduced in intercontinental PTAs is more likely to pollinate other regions and diffuse successfully.[19] This is also echoed by negotiators, who underline the importance of being exposed to different ways of linking trade and the environment in PTAs (interview with official from Chile, 2017).

Learning mechanisms can facilitate the diffusion of environmental provisions, not only within regions, but also from high-income to low-income countries (Postnikov, 2020). Trade policy officials from the South and the epistemic community of 'Southern trade intellectuals' (Scott, 2015) frequently communicate with their northern counterparts in joint bodies and other international institutions, as well as their broader networks. The resulting learning processes can promote the diffusion of environmental provisions, even in the absence of the bargaining power differential typical of North-South trade relations (e.g., in South-South PTAs).[20] In the light of such learning mechanisms, Gamso and Postnikov (2022) show that developing countries adopt North-South PTA templates and argue that they do so because of policy learning from prior negotiations with developed countries rather than in response to competition pressures or coercion.

Interestingly, environmental provisions designed by economically powerful countries do not diffuse more frequently than other environmental provisions (Morin et al., 2019a). Moreover, the involvement of the EU or the US does not

---

[19] This is in line with the literature on network analysis (e.g., Cao, 2010) and the literature on contagion (e.g., Baldwin & Jaimovich, 2012).

[20] Similar mechanisms have been found to be relevant for the diffusion of regional integration (Jetschke & Lenz, 2013).

lead to a higher frequency of diffusion in PTAs that do not involve economic superpowers, other things being equal. Overall, these results challenge the commonly held view that power asymmetry is the main mechanism in diffusion patterns. That does not mean that powerful states never push less powerful states to include environmental provisions in exchange for market access or that power asymmetries do not play a role (see also Sections 4 and 5). It simply means that the negotiation power of the country behind innovation does not significantly influence the diffusion of environmental provisions in later PTAs between third parties.

Instead, countries regarded as credible environmental leaders often contribute to the diffusion of environmental provisions. As environmentally credible countries are considered 'norm entrepreneurs', they can encourage others to adopt their standards (Finnemore & Sikkink, 1998). When environmentally credible countries include environmental provisions in their PTAs, it signals to other countries that the policy innovation is important and expected to be effective. Countries seeking to strengthen their environmental credibility tend to emulate countries they regard as credible. This in turn promotes the diffusion of innovative provisions in the trade regime complex.

For example, the EU is considered a credible climate-policy leader. It decided to systematically refer to the Paris Agreement in all its PTAs, starting with its 2018 agreement with Japan. This announcement will likely act as a benchmark for other countries concerned with climate change. In fact, countries around the world have started inserting references to the Paris Agreement and other types of climate provisions in their PTAs. Recent agreements that incorporate a reference to the Paris Agreement include the 2020 agreement between Chile and Equator and the 2020 agreement between Canada and the UK. At the same time, as mentioned above, despite the presence of numerous PTAs that include comprehensive environmental chapters, many still fail to specifically address climate change or do so in a superficial manner only (Brandi et al., forthcoming).

Provisions That Are Widely Diffused

In our large-n analysis on the diffusion of environmental provisions in PTAs, we did not only assess the initial conditions that are likely to kick-start diffusion processes but also investigated the types of provisions that have a higher likelihood of spreading (Morin et al., 2019a). The empirical evidence indicates that defensive provisions offering innovative solutions for safeguarding countries' regulatory space tend to diffuse more frequently. This finding suggests that many countries prioritize the protection of their right to regulate environmental issues and shield themselves from potential trade disputes. Additionally, we find that provisions focusing on specific environmental issue and those related to policy coherence are more likely to diffuse. Provisions related to development and implementation also tend to diffuse broadly.

Some environmental provisions have never been replicated and remain the sole province of one country and its PTAs (Morin & Gauthier-Nadeau, 2017). New provisions continue to emerge, meaning that differentiation within the trade governance system can be maintained (Morin et al., 2017). Of the 298 types of provisions covered by TREND, 48 are found in only five or fewer trade agreements. For example, the commitment to conduct environmental impact assessments has not been broadly diffused, despite its potential. Clear commitments relating to the liberalization of environmental goods and services have also failed to spread much. More than seventy PTAs refer to the benefits of liberalizing environmental goods and services, but only a limited number incorporate any specific commitments.

Having discussed the diffusion of environmental provisions around the world and the limits of this diffusion, we now turn to the analysis of the effects of these provisions. In the context of the North-South dynamics outlined above, we put a particular spotlight on developing countries.

7 Effects of Environmental Provisions in PTAs

This section investigates the implications of including environmental provisions in trade agreements. Specifically, we analyse the environmental and economic effects of such provisions in PTAs and explore the trade-offs and synergies between economic growth and environmental protection, drawing upon the theoretical frameworks introduced in Section 2. We first examine the environmental impact of environmental provisions in PTAs, and then evaluate their economic implications. One question we address is whether the inclusion of environmental provisions in PTAs inevitably results in trade-offs between international trade and environmental protection, with one coming at the expense of the other. Alternatively, we explore whether such provisions can lead to synergies, where trade and environmental protection mutually reinforce each other. By understanding the relationship between trade and the environment in PTAs, we aim to shed light on the potential of these agreements to contribute to sustainable development.

Environmental Effects

Several studies suggest that environmental provisions in trade agreements have positive environmental implications. They find that these provisions are associated with lower CO_2 emissions (Francois et al., 2023; Martínez-Zarzoso & Oueslati, 2018) and a reduction in air pollution (Baghdadi et al., 2013; Zhou et al., 2017). Moreover, while trade liberalization tends to increase deforestation

(Abman & Lundberg, 2020), including specific provisions to protect forests or biodiversity counterbalances the net increases in forest loss detected in otherwise comparable PTAs that do not have this type of provision (Abman et al., 2021). Recent research on fist stocks suggests that trade agreements tend to have a negative effect on their status but that including fisheries-related environmental provisions in PTAs offsets this negative impact (Bayramoglu et al., 2023). Moreover, membership in the CPTPP, which includes a stringent provision on the reduction fishery subsidies that harm the environment, is associated with a more than 20 per cent increase in environmentally friendly subsidies compared to non-members (Rickard, 2022).[21] Environmental provisions have also been found to improve overall environmental performance (Bastiaens & Postnikov, 2017).

However, establishing a causal relationship between treaty adoption and reduction in environmental degradation is circuitous. Previous large-n research on treaty effectiveness has assessed the distant impact of environmental content in trade agreements on environmental quality. However, the exact causal mechanism, if any, remains unclear. For this reason, we focus on the more direct links between the conclusion of a PTA and the adoption of environmental regulations.

Our findings show that the signing of PTAs with environmental provisions is linked to the adoption of domestic environmental regulations (Brandi et al., 2019). Figure 14 illustrates this correlation. As the data shows, the relationship between PTAs and domestic environmental regulations is particularly strong in developing

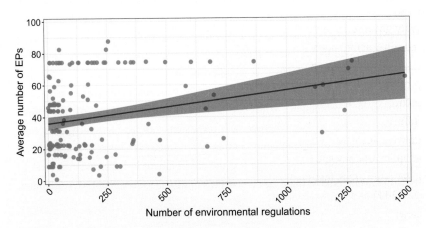

Figure 14 Number of environmental regulations and average number of environmental provisions in PTAs (2010–2020)

---

[21] In New Zealand, for instance, almost all of the general fisheries subsidies are allocated towards sustainable initiatives, including those that assist in managing sustainable catch limits and offset related expenses.

countries. Due to economic inequalities, developing countries are more likely to implement regulatory changes to gain access to their new trading partners' markets (Baccini & Urpelainen, 2014) or to benefit from assistance for capacity building (VanDeveer & Dabelko, 2001). In addition, as developing countries typically have less ambitious environmental policies than high-income countries, they must catch up to comply with new treaty obligations.

Our analysis also suggests that PTAs are more effective at promoting environmental regulations on certain environmental issues than on others (Brandi et al., 2019). This is not surprising given that the cost/benefit ratio of implementing measures varies across environmental issues, and countries tend to prioritize the least costly or the most beneficial regulations in the short term (Sprinz & Vaahtoranta, 1994). For instance, regulating local environmental challenges, such as water, air, and soil quality, generates more direct benefits than regulating global common resources, such as the atmosphere (Mitchell, 2006). While some types of regulations lead to high marginal abatement costs, such as fishing quotas, others generate substantial social co-benefits, such as health benefits due to better air quality in cities. Political economic factors may also intervene in this causal process. For example, marginalized populations might not be able to successfully oppose the establishment of nature reserves in remote areas, whereas well-organized interest groups are better equipped to challenge regulations that have a negative impact on their industries.

Let us now consider different examples. Measures to protect freshwater and air quality are typically characterized by low regulatory costs. They can be effectively governed at the regional level, generate large co-benefits (e.g., health), and mobilize actors such as NGOs, businesses, and local authorities in favour of environmental protection. However, measures to mitigate climate change and protect fish stocks are less attractive for decision-makers. Considerable investments are required to generate distant benefits, and industrial losers tend to be influential in domestic policymaking (Colgan et al., 2021). This explains why the link between the conclusion of a PTA with environmental provisions and the adoption of domestic environmental regulation is more pronounced in the case of local issue areas that generate substantial social co-benefits, such as air quality (SDG 11) or clean water (SDG 6), compared to regulations targeting global issue areas with higher social costs, such as climate change (SDG 13).

Overall, these insights suggest that concluding PTAs with environmental provisions can favour regulatory changes for some environmental issues. This finding supports existing research that indicates a positive link between environmental content in trade agreements and environmental protection. However, this finding does not necessarily imply that the newly introduced environmental regulations are stricter. There is no guarantee that they will be enforced or generate improved environmental outcomes. Nonetheless, we consider it reasonable to assume that most PTAs analysed in our study require regulatory change, and that such regulatory change is a crucial step for improving environmental protection.

Foreign Direct Investment (FDI)

The question of whether environmental provisions in PTAs impact business activities and how investors react to them is complex. On the one hand, stronger environmental regulations could potentially increase operational and compliance costs for multinational companies (MNCs), which could hinder their entry or expansion into a country. However, on the other hand, environmental provisions can also encourage FDI between PTA partners by reducing transaction costs and increasing productivity. Moreover, MNCs with strong corporate responsibility and social awareness policies may prefer countries with explicit commitments to environmental issues in their PTAs, providing a competitive advantage for countries with stronger environmental regulations.

Similar to Vogel's (1997) perspective on the 'trading up' of environmental regulations via international trade, Prakash and Potoski (2007) find that FDI can act as a mechanism for the 'investing up' of corporate environmental practices. Research on LDCs finds that even FDI from these countries can improve the environmental practices of host country firms, suggesting that LDC companies regard it as financially beneficial to underlining their commitment to environmental protection to consumers, investors, employees, and potential business partners (Zeng & Eastin, 2012).

What do empirical analyses reveal about the effect of PTAs with environmental provisions on FDI? Existing research suggests that environmental provisions have heterogeneous effects across sectors in the US, with a reduction in FDI in polluting sectors but an increase in environmentally clean sectors (Lechner, 2018). However, the effects of environmental provisions on FDI across countries are unclear. One recent study found that non-trade provisions, including environmental provisions, have a negative effect on FDI flows, particularly in middle- and low-income countries (Di Ubaldo & Gasiorek, 2022). Another study found no empirical evidence that adding environmental provisions to a PTA decreases bilateral FDI (see Rojas-Romagosa, 2020). Therefore, the literature provides inconclusive findings on the effects of environmental provisions in PTAs on FDI.

Trade Flows

Existing studies suggest that PTAs can increase trade flows, enhance productivity, and generate higher incomes (Baccini, 2019; Winters & Martuscelli, 2014), which are key for achieving several SDGs. Moreover, existing studies suggest that deeper PTAs create more trade than shallow agreements (Baier et al., 2014; Dür et al., 2014). However, it is unclear how these positive economic effects are impacted by environmental provisions. In fact, there are concerns that environmental provisions can be in tension with the PTA's main goal because they reduce trade flows. Trade and environment interlinkages are crucial, but we know little about the economic impacts of environmental provisions.

To examine this question, we investigate the effects of environmental provisions on the exports of parties to trade agreements. Our research finds that while some developing countries are worried that high-income countries will use environmental provisions in PTAs to promote 'green protectionism', the inclusion of environmental provisions in PTAs does not significantly lessen their overall positive trade-generating effect (Brandi et al., 2020). Environmental provisions slightly lessen the overall positive trade-generating effect of PTAs, if at all. This finding was borderline in terms of statistical significance (Berger et al., 2020). With a slightly different sample, we find that including environmental provisions does not significantly reduce the trade-generating effects of PTAs in a statistically significant way (Brandi et al., 2020). This suggests that environmental provisions in PTAs do not involve any trade-off between the environmental and economic dimensions of sustainable development.

Trade in Environmental Goods

We assess how environmental provisions affect the trade composition. Do they promote environmentally friendly trade relations? To answer this question, we set out to unravel the effects of different environmental provisions on dirty and green goods (Brandi et al., 2020). We refer to goods as 'dirty' when they generate high pollution abatement costs (such as cement) and as 'green' when they reduce or remedy environmental damage (such as wind turbines).

Dirty and green sectors play a key role in ongoing trade-environment debates about the possible upsurge of pollution havens in developing countries. The so-called Pollution Haven Hypothesis suggests that the reduction of trade and investment barriers triggers the relocation of environmentally harmful production from (high-income) countries with stringent environmental regulations to (developing) countries with less stringent environmental regulations (Copeland & Taylor, 1994). On the other hand, the so-called Porter hypothesis outlines a very different perspective: environmental regulation does not threaten competitiveness but rather generates incentives for companies to be innovative, which increases productivity (Porter, 1991; Porter & van de Linde, 1995). Thus, PTAs that promote environmental regulations can encourage environmentally friendly technologies and foster green trade flows. Several studies present empirical evidence to support the Porter hypothesis (Cohen & Tubb, 2018; Mealy & Teytelboym, 2020) and the Pollution Haven hypothesis (Cherniwchan, 2017; Kolcava et al., 2019), but findings are inconclusive.

As PTA environmental provisions are heterogeneous, they are likely to have diverse effects on trade across sectors. Some provisions may limit trade, whereas others may foster trade flows. Therefore, we distinguish between liberal and trade-restrictive environmental provisions and assess their effects at the sectoral level (Brandi et al., 2020).

Trade-restrictive provisions are intended to reduce environmentally unsustainable trade flows. First, countries with stringent environmental policies can use these provisions to level the playing field with countries with weak environmental regulations (Bhagwati, 1995). For instance, environmental provisions may require parties to strengthen their environmental protection, which may reduce the competitive advantage of countries with less stringent regulations. Second, other trade-restrictive environmental provisions are intended to limit environmentally harmful trade flow. For example, the Caribbean Community agreed 'to protect the region from the harmful effects of hazardous materials transported, generated, disposed of, or shipped through or within the Community' (CARICOM, 2001).

Liberal provisions, however, aim to promote green trade. They include provisions that specifically demand a reduction in trade barriers for environmental goods and services (see Figure 15). For instance, the EU-Georgia PTA (2014) demands that parties 'facilitate the removal of obstacles to trade or investment concerning goods and services of particular relevance to climate change mitigation, such as sustainable renewable energy and energy efficient products and services'. The 2013 PTA between New Zealand and Taiwan calls for the removal of all tariffs on environmental goods. Liberal environmental provisions also include provisions that foster international standards or harmonize domestic measures. Liberal environmental provisions that strengthen economic openness can stimulate the diffusion of environmentally friendly technologies and innovations (Prakash & Potoski, 2006), thereby strengthening the competitiveness of green sectors.

When the distinction between liberal and restrictive environmental provisions is taken into account, the central question is: how do these different types of provisions affect trade in green goods, which reduce or remedy environmental damage, and trade in 'dirty' goods, which pollute.

Two key findings emerge from our empirical analysis (Brandi et al., 2020). First, we find that environmental provisions in PTAs reduce 'dirty' exports. High-income countries focus on environmental provisions that curb exports from polluting industries in developing countries. This reflects the concerns of both environmental NGOs and the private sector. Businesses in high-income countries are keen to avoid competition from developing countries, whereas

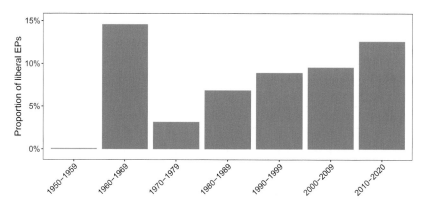

Figure 15 Bar chart of the per cent of liberal environmental provisions in PTAs per decade

environmental NGOs strive to prevent pollution havens in developing countries. Consequently, high-income countries have strong incentives to shape environmental provisions that limit developing countries' dirty exports.

Second, we find that environmental provisions in PTAs boost green exports. They increase the competitiveness of green sectors (Mealy & Teytelboym, 2020) and facilitate exports of green goods. This amplifies the win-win options for the developing countries, encouraging them to insert environmental provisions in their PTAs to develop synergies between the economic and environmental dimensions of sustainable development.

We also find that these effects are stronger in developing countries that already have a strong environmental record and are on the path to green transformation than in developing countries with lower standards. These countries seem to have the greater capacity to green their exports in response to PTA environmental provisions. One of the main reasons for this is that socio-technical development is typically path-dependent and specializing in green sectors increases the likelihood of future green specialization (Mealy & Teytelboym, 2020). Therefore, firms in countries with more stringent environmental regulations can respond swiftly to new environmental provisions and adapt their production patterns and export structures more easily than firms from other developing countries.

Our empirical findings show an increasing share of green goods in the exports of developing countries. This is consistent with the Porter hypothesis, which states that stricter environmental regulations stimulate the competitiveness of green sectors. In addition, our findings suggest that environmental provisions and the stricter environmental regulations they induce may counteract the potential effects of pollution havens. Looking ahead, it would be helpful to shed more light on the specific channels through which environmental provisions PTAs affect trade flows. For instance, environmental provisions in PTAs can influence firms' ability to produce different products, engage in global value chains (GVCs), and access new markets.

Our empirical evidence highlights the critical role of PTA designs from a policy perspective. We discovered that PTA provisions could be utilized as policy instruments to promote synergies between trade and the environment. In addition to using these win-win options, decision-makers should ensure that they include provisions that necessitate environmental capacity building in developing countries to promote sustainable development and ensure that these countries can effectively implement and comply with environmental provisions in trade agreements.

Overall, we discovered that there is no general trade-off between environmental and economic effects when environmental provisions are included in PTAs. These provisions do not significantly reduce the exports of developing countries. Instead, they can promote trade and green the ensuing trade flows, creating potential win-win situations for developing countries. As a result, environmental provisions have the potential to produce trade benefits for developing countries while simultaneously contributing to their transition toward sustainability. At the same time, recent research (Hoekman et al., 2023) suggests that environmental provisions in PTAs might be associated with an increase in trade in energy-intensive products (but without distinguishing the effects of different types of provisions). Moreover, the positive impacts of including environmental provisions in PTAs might be context-specific and both researchers and policy-makers should always take account of the particular setting at stake when tackling the interface between trade and the environment.

8 Multilateralizing Environmental Provisions

The interplay between trade and the environment is more dynamic at the bilateral and regional levels than at the multilateral level of the WTO. PTAs serve as laboratories in which trade negotiators experiment with new provisions before they are incorporated into the WTO rulebook (Baldwin & Low, 2009). This section goes beyond the dynamic developments at the bilateral and regional levels and discusses broader implications for greening trade governance at the multilateral level. We examine various policy scenarios that have the potential to achieve multilateral progress on the trade-environment interface.

Understanding the prospects for multilateralizing environmental provisions is essential as it can make a significant contribution to environmental governance. First, environmental provisions have positive environmental effects and should be included in WTO agreements. Their multilateralization would broaden their scope of application and enhance their effectiveness. Moreover, the WTO's multilateral forum is preferable to PTAs for developing countries because they can form bargaining coalitions (Narlikar, 2003) and there are fewer power asymmetries. Finally, the multilateralization may improve enforcement by subjecting environmental provisions to the WTO's stringent dispute settlement mechanism.[22]

The reduction of fishery subsidies is an excellent example of how environmental provisions in PTAs can promote multilateral progress in the WTO. Despite more than two decades of multilateral negotiations on fishery subsidies, the WTO Agreement on Fisheries Subsidies was only adopted in 2022. The CPTPP, which became effective in 2018 and includes several major fishing nations, contains innovative provisions on fishery subsidies that helped pave the way for the eventual conclusion of the recent WTO Agreement. Some of the text from the CPTPP, including the definition of fish, is now present in the newly adopted WTO deal and has directly influenced these new multilateral rules.

This illustrates how experimenting with environmental provisions in the context of PTAs can help to overcome gridlock in the multilateral trading system, thereby allowing for more flexibility and adaptability in the overall trade regime complex. By exploring how multilateralization can be achieved through PTAs, we can gain insights into how trade and environmental policy can be more effectively integrated, leading to more sustainable trade governance.

Prospects for Multilateralization

What are the prospects for the multilateralization of PTA provisions? They partly depend on the willingness of major trading powers, such as the EU and the US, to reach a multilateral agreement. In Section 3, we outline how the EU approach to including environmental provisions in PTAs differs from the US approach. In Figure 16, each vertical line represents a different type of environmental provision from the TREND codebook. This shows that a number of environmental provisions appear primarily or solely in either EU or US agreements. Historically, the US aimed to level the playing field, favour public participation, and protect its regulatory sovereignty. In contrast, the EU focused more on achieving policy coherence at the trade, environment, and development interface.

In recent years, negotiators across the Atlantic have increasingly agreed on a common set of environmental provisions (Morin & Rochette, 2017). EU and US negotiators have learned and borrowed from each other. As mentioned in

---

[22] The WTO's Appellate Body is still paralysed due to disagreement over the appointment of new arbitrators, but the Interim Appeal Arbitration Arrangement, introduced by a group of 16 WTO members, provides a temporary solution for appealing the WTO panel's decisions before an arbitration tribunal.

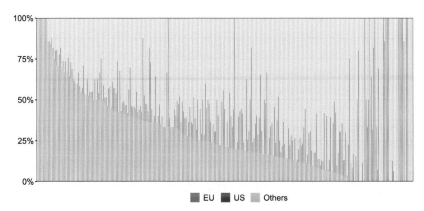

Figure 16 The distribution of environmental provisions in PTAs

Section 6 (see Figure 12), the EU and US approaches are converging. More recently, EU PTAs have become more American, with more stringent enforcement rules and better protection for regulatory sovereignty. US PTAs have become more European with provisions that govern technology transfer and fine-grained provisions on specific environmental issues (Morin & Rochette, 2017). The European and American approaches are by no means irreconcilable and can be effectively combined. The convergence between the EU and the US models increases the likelihood of finding common ground among key players in the trading system. In turn, this improves the prospects of multilateralizing environmental provisions.

How might major emerging market players, such as China or India, react to initiatives to multilateralize PTA measures? On the one hand, some developing countries and emerging markets may view multilateralizing environmental provisions in PTAs as a form of 'green protectionism' (Draper et al., 2017, p. ii). They may also argue that multilateralizing environmental provisions in PTAs could disproportionately affect their economies, as they may not have the resources or technology to comply with strict environmental standards. However, many developing countries and emerging markets recognize the importance of environmental protection and sustainability. They may welcome initiatives to multilateralize environmental provisions in PTAs. This could also help prevent countries from turning into pollution havens (Copeland & Taylor, 1994; see also Section 7). Furthermore, as indicated in Section 3, not all developing countries oppose the integration of trade and environment. In fact, some developing countries lead the way in the inclusion of environmental provisions in PTAs.

Hence, the question is not whether developing and emerging economies would endorse the inclusion of environmental clauses in a future WTO agreement, but instead which specific types of environmental provisions are most likely to garner support from a significant number of WTO members. As discussed in the next section, the prospects for multilateralizing environmental content are substantially improved by the new dynamic on trade and the environment in the WTO. Several developing and emerging economies are promoting this new multilateral dynamic, including major emerging market players such as China.

A New Momentum at the WTO

The multilateralization of PTA provisions may seem unlikely, given the existing legislative gridlock in the WTO. However, recently, a new dynamic has emerged in the WTO context at the trade-environment interface. After the (failed) negotiations on the Environmental Goods Agreement (EGA), a small group of countries, the Friends Advancing Sustainable Trade (FAST Group), including Canada, Costa Rica, the EU, Norway, and Switzerland, drafted a joint statement on trade and environmental sustainability. The aim of the FAST group was to ensure that its statement appealed to developing countries. For example, it focused on the circular economy, plastic pollution, agricultural issues, and greening Aid for Trade rather than just market access for environmental goods and services. The group was keen to involve developing countries from the outset and, thus, to move away from the 'rich men's club' of the EGA negotiations. The idea was for discussions to be as inclusive and ambitious as possible (interview with official at the EU Commission, DG TRADE, 6 September 2021).

In 2020, fifty-three WTO members launched a novel process 'to collaborate, prioritize, and advance discussions on trade and environmental sustainability' (WTO, 2020). In 2021, the new Trade and Environmental Sustainability Structured Discussions (TESSD) issued a ministerial statement acknowledging 'sustainable development and the protection and preservation of the environment' as 'fundamental goals of the WTO'. It recognizes the role of international trade policy in supporting environmental objectives and advancing sustainable consumption and production (WTO, 2021).[23] The ministers agreed to identify activities in areas of common interest in order to: 'expand opportunities for environmentally sustainable trade'; launch 'dedicated discussions' to 'explore ways in which trade-related climate measures can contribute to climate and environmental objectives'; explore avenues to facilitate trade in environmental goods and services to meet climate and environmental goals; and 'encourage capacity-building and technical assistance on trade and environmental sustainability' (WTO, 2021).

---

[23] The statement underlines that Structured Discussions 'are not meant to duplicate other initiatives in the WTO' and sees its activities as complementary to existing work, such as in the WTO Committee on Trade and Environment.

In addition, two other ministerial statements were launched at the WTO, respectively on plastic pollution and fossil fuel subsidy reform. These initiatives are promising with regard to making progress on trade and the environment in the multilateral context. Indeed, they are supported by a wide range of countries from around the world, including many developing countries, such as Chad and the Gambia, as well as major emerging economies such as Mexico and Brazil. This is remarkable, as these countries used to be opposed to discussing environmental issues in the WTO over the past decades.

By now, the TESSD countries represent more than 85 per cent of world trade, and more countries are joining to participate. In 2021, both the US and China joined the structured discussions and became co-sponsors of this plurilateral initiative. During a meeting of the Committee on Trade and Environment (CTE) in 2022, China 'expressed support for the WTO as the main channel for coordinating trade policies in pursuit of cooperation in global climate governance'.[24]

This new dynamic in the WTO at the trade-environment interface, which includes key players such as the EU, the US, and China, represents a window of opportunity for multilateralizing environmental provisions. This highlights the importance of assessing the prospects for further progress at the multilateral level, as well as the need to identify the specific types of environmental provisions most likely to be multilateralized, that is, added to the WTO rule book.

Multilateral Scenarios

To examine which environmental provisions are more likely to be multilateralized, we compare five multilateralization scenarios that outline potential multilateral agreements incorporating some of the environmental provisions now included in PTAs. Each of these scenarios are only ideal type,[25] unlikely to actually arise in practice. Nevertheless, the diverse scenarios can be used to further our knowledge and facilitate exchanges of existing practices and the likely content of future multilateral agreements (Morin et al., 2019b). The 'routine scenario' combines the most frequent environmental provisions; the 'consensual scenario' includes the provisions that are acceptable for many WTO members; the 'trendy scenario' includes the most widespread recent provisions; the 'power-game scenario' includes provisions that are backed by

---

[24] www.wto.org/english/news_e/news22_e/envir_21oct22_e.htm. During this meeting, India, among other members, raised concerns over the 'increasing use of unilateral measures impacting trade which are sought to be justified as environmental measures'. While India has not joined the TESSD, this statement suggests that the country is interested in using the multilateral forum to address the trade-environment interface.

[25] The concept of the 'ideal type', first introduced by the German sociologist Max Weber, refers to a conceptual tool that is used to simplify and clarify complex social phenomena and provides a benchmark against which actual social phenomena can be evaluated.

both the US and the EU; the 'appropriate scenario' includes provisions that are typically incorporated in agreements with broad membership. Building on these scenarios, we investigate how WTO members can advance the inclusion of environmental content in the multilateral trade system.

For this purpose, we identify a possible Common Ground Agreement that combines the five multilateralization scenarios. The different environmental provisions in the agreement could provide a common basis for multilateralization. The Common Ground Agreement includes a number of general environmental provisions (e.g., clauses that establish mechanisms for cooperation among PTA partners). Moreover, it contains several provisions related to specific environmental issues such as hazardous waste, forest conservation, and greenhouse gas emissions. If these provisions became multilateral, it would represent significant progress for the trade-environment interplay. The Common Ground Agreement also includes a number of fish-related provisions, some of which have helped pave the way for the WTO Agreement on Fisheries Subsidies. Moreover, it contains provisions that aim to harmonize technical environmental regulations and improve the enforcement of domestic environmental laws. In addition, it includes provisions on public participation, as well as development-related provisions on capacity building and technology transfer. Table 1 summarizes the environmental provisions of the Common Ground Agreement. It shows the number of PTAs that incorporate these provisions, the number of countries subscribed to them, and the share of PTAs that contains them. It also includes examples of these types of environmental provisions from existing PTAs.

Promoting Multilateral Environmental Agreements

Preferential trade agreements also strengthen multilateralism because they entail an increasing number of references to MEAs (Morin & Bialais, 2018). The share of PTAs that refer to MEAs and the average number of references per PTA have risen over time. It is now common for trade agreements to refer to six or more MEAs. As shown in Figure 17, the range of MEAs cited in trade agreements is also expanding. The most frequently cited MEAs include CITES (1973), the United Nations Framework Convention on Climate Change (UNFCCC) (1992), and the Convention on Biological Diversity (1992).

Incorporating references to MEAs in trade agreements can help strengthen environmental governance and enhance the effectiveness of MEAs in three different ways (Morin & Bialais, 2018): First, some references to MEAs clarify the hierarchy of provisions in PTAs and MEAs. This improves the coherence of

Table 1 Environmental provisions with high multilateralization potential

Provisions	Example	Number of PTAs including the provision	Number of countries that subscribed to the provision	Per cent of PTAs including the provision (2015–2020)
States should provide for high levels of environmental protection	New Zealand-Thailand (2005): 'The Participants reaffirm their [. . .] commitments, as global citizens, to high levels of environmental protection.'	89	102	47.9
States should enhance, strengthen, improve levels of environmental protection	Chile-US (2003): 'Each Party [. . .] shall strive to continue to improve those [environmental] laws.'	86	157	45.2
Binding obligations to enforce environmental measures	NAAEC (1992): 'Each Party shall effectively enforce its environmental laws and regulations through appropriate governmental action [. . .]'	113	108	50.7
Environmental goods and services	Canada-Colombia (2008): 'The Parties shall encourage the promotion of the trade and investment of environmental goods and services.'	76	154	37.0

The parties shall encourage the transfer of environmental technologies	Brunei-Japan (2007): 'Each Party shall: [...] encourage favourable conditions for the transfer and dissemination of technologies that contribute to the protection of environment [...]'	58	96	20.6
The parties shall engage the public in activities undertaken to implement this agreement	Australia-US (2004) 'Each Party shall provide an opportunity for its public, which may include national advisory committees, to provide views, recommendations, or advice on matters related to the implementation of this section, and shall make available such views, recommendations, or advice to the other Party and, as appropriate, to the public in accordance with its law.'	77	157	43.8
Procedures for harmonizing technical environmental regulations	Canada-Chile (1996) 'The Council shall strengthen cooperation on the development and continuing improvement of environmental laws and regulations, including by [...] establishing a process for developing recommendations on greater compatibility of environmental technical regulations, standards and conformity assessment procedures [...].'	63	163	17.8

Table 1 (cont.)

Provisions	Example	Number of PTAs including the provision	Number of countries that subscribed to the provision	Per cent of PTAs including the provision (2015 −2020)
Cooperation on the protection of forests	Brunei-Japan (2007): '[T]he Parties, recognising the importance of securing stable food supply and of sustainable development of agriculture, forestry and fisheries, shall cooperate in the field of agriculture, forestry and fisheries [. . .].'	82	153	39.7
Management of domestic waste	Bulgaria-EC (1993): 'Cooperation shall concern: − waste reduction [. . .] and safe disposal.'	85	116	27.4
Reduction of greenhouse gas emissions	EC-Israel Euro-Med (1995): 'The Parties consider that global warming and the depletion of fossil fuel sources are a serious threat to mankind. The Parties shall therefore cooperate with a view to developing sources of renewable energy [. . .].'	52	138	34.3

Conservation of fishery resources	CARICOM revised (2001): 'The Community [. . .] shall promote the development, management and conservation of the fisheries resources in and among the Member States on a sustainable basis.'	93	159	39.7
Control and prevention of marine pollution	USMCA (2018): 'The Parties recognize the importance of taking action to prevent and reduce marine litter, including plastic litter and microplastics, in order to preserve human health and marine and coastal ecosystems, prevent the loss of biodiversity, and mitigate marine litter's costs and impacts.'	88	163	32.9
Developed countries shall provide capacity building to developing country parties	Peru–US (2008): 'The Parties are committed to work cooperatively [. . .] including through capacity-building and other joint initiatives to promote the sustainable management of Peru's forest resources.'	109	168	37.0

Table 1 (cont.)

Provisions	Example	Number of PTAs including the provision	Number of countries that subscribed to the provision	Per cent of PTAs including the provision (2015–2020)
Prevent harmful fisheries subsidies	Trans-pacific Partnership (2016) (predecessor of CPTPP): 'The Parties recognize that the implementation of a fisheries management system that is designed to prevent overfishing and overcapacity and to promote the recovery of overfished stocks must include the control, reduction and eventual elimination of all subsidies that contribute to overfishing and overcapacity.'	6	18	8.2
Combat illegal fishing	China-Peru (2009): 'The objective of cooperation on fishery will be to […] to facilitate […] the conservation of natural resources, under the approach of responsible fishing. […] The Parties will develop fishery through […] combat of illegal, unreported and unregulated fishing.'	34	91	30.1

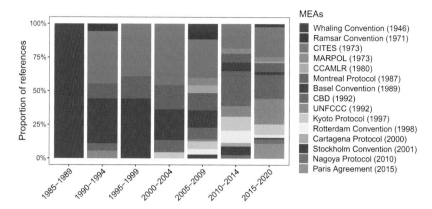

Figure 17 References to MEAs in PTAs

global governance by averting inconsistencies and by enhancing mutual reinforcement. Second, some PTAs demand the ratification of specific environmental agreements. For instance, the Common Market for Eastern and Southern Africa (COMESA) requires its members to accede to the UNFCCC. Consequently, the seventeen COMESA members that had not yet done so ratified the UNFCCC shortly after COMESA was set up. Third, PTAs can require the implementation of specific MEAs, such as the Paris Agreement. The trade agreement concluded between the EU and Japan in 2017 was the first to do so. In sum, PTAs can strengthen multilateral environmental governance. References to MEAs can expand MEA membership, accelerate their entry into force, and offer further incentives for implementation. Moreover, introducing references to MEAs into PTAs can enhance the coherence of international law, thereby addressing the challenge of fragmentation (introduced in Section 2).

Nevertheless, the effect of references to MEAs in PTAs remains limited. To determine whether PTAs actually increased MEA membership, Laurens and Morin (2019) compared the signature date of the PTA with the ratification date of the MEA to which it refers. They found that 84 per cent of PTAs with a provision on the implementation or ratification of a major MEA are concluded between countries that had ratified the MEA beforehand. Only twenty-nine PTAs (or 4 per cent of the total number of PTAs analysed), include a rule stating that some or all of the provisions of at least one MEA should prevail in the event of a conflict with PTA provisions. In fact, some trade negotiators remain sceptical about the links between MEAs and PTAs. They regard them as different mechanisms that should remain distinct (Interview with official from Chile, 2017).

Multilateralism is desirable from a normative perspective. Powerful nations are less likely to have the upper hand in a multilateral setting. Weaker countries can promote their positions by joining bargaining coalitions. We believe that it is important to safeguard the needs and interests of developing countries and less powerful players in global governance. Therefore, multilateralism should be safeguarded and strengthened as much as possible. As suggested in this Element, bilateral and regional agreements can pave the way for multilateralism and positively contribute to global governance.

9 Conclusions and Policy Recommendations

This Element explores the growing interlinkages between trade and environmental governance and presents a key finding: that well-designed trade governance approaches, including trade agreements, can serve as powerful tools for enhancing environmental protection and promoting sustainable development. Contrary to the traditional view that trade liberalization undermines environmental governance, the interplay between trade and the environment within preferential trade governance can offer opportunities to strengthen environmental governance.

Overarching Findings

The empirical insights presented in this Element have significant implications for the trade-environment interface. Firstly, our research highlights the benefits of experimenting with the trade-environment interface. Second, it reveals the existence of significant gaps and untapped potentials that require attention. Third, our findings indicate that linking trade and the environment can lead to mutually reinforcing outcomes rather than tensions. Fourth, our analysis of the impact of specific provisions identifies the types of provisions that are most effective in promoting environmental protection. Finally, our empirical insights can inform discussions at the WTO and other international and transnational forums regarding how to use the trade policy toolbox to address environmental issues.

By investigating the nature, drivers, effects, and future prospects of EPs in PTAs, we explored the following four questions, which cut across different sections in the Element:

1. How does global governance at the trade and environment interface contribute to environmental performance?

We have demonstrated that effective governance at the trade-environment interface is crucial for achieving SDGs. International treaties play a significant role in reinforcing environmental governance. In particular, our analysis shows that environmental provisions in trade agreements, which are becoming more comprehensive and detailed, can improve environmental governance in various ways. For instance, they can facilitate compliance with MEAs, promote environmental aid and capacity building in developing countries, empower environmental NGOs and civil society, encourage the adoption of new environmental policies, and boost the trade of green goods. Thus, when designed effectively, trade-environment interlinkages can contribute to improving environmental governance and promoting environmental protection.

2. To what extent does governance at the trade and environment interface lead to trade-offs between the economic and environmental dimensions of sustainable development?

Managing the interface between trade and the environment involves striking a balance between trade-offs and identifying synergies that can benefit sustainable development. This Element demonstrated that trade agreements can leverage important synergies through environmental provisions and promote policy coherence for sustainable development. For instance, provisions that boost the export of environmental goods can generate both economic and environmental gains. Nevertheless, many potential synergies remain unexplored, such as phasing out fossil fuel subsidies, liberalizing environmental services, and increasing access to patented environmental technologies. Countries and regional entities committed to policy coherence must ensure that their trade policies adequately consider sustainable development impacts.

3. To what extent are high-income countries taking advantage of power imbalances to impose their views on the trade and environment interface?

Our Element highlights the vulnerable positions of developing countries and the need to consider power dynamics carefully. They may face pressure to accept environmental provisions that do not align with their own priorities. However, the diffusion of environmental provisions is not driven solely by powerful countries. Environmental leaders such as Peru have successfully introduced their environmental priorities in PTAs, which are now diffusing globally.

Our research suggests that aid commitments can help achieve a balanced solution. Recipients with relatively poor environmental performance receive greater aid commitment, and we find a positive association between the number of environmental provisions in PTAs and aggregate aid after signing new PTAs. This finding suggests that aid can effectively facilitate the transition to greener economies.

However, aid commitments do not always result in actual aid transfers. It remains unclear whether the inclusion of aid and capacity-building provisions in PTAs increases environmental aid flow. When environmental provisions are included in PTAs, developing countries face legal and political pressure to enhance their environmental protection. This arguably reduces the need for donor countries to use environmental aid incentives to achieve their environmental goals. In other words, environmental obligations in PTAs could be used as a 'policy substitute' for environmental aid to improve environmental protection in developing countries. This raises questions regarding the enforcement of high-income countries' commitments to providing environmental aid.

4. As more environmental provisions are included in more trade agreements, what are the implications for the fragmented nature of trade and environment interlinkages and regime complexes?

While many scholars criticize the fragmentation of trade and environmental governance, our Element provides a more optimistic perspective on the interplay between trade and the environment. Despite the challenges posed by the 'spaghetti bowl' of PTAs, we argue that the fragmented nature of regime complexes can actually improve the resilience and adaptability of global governance. PTAs can help overcome the stalemate in the WTO and allow experimentation with environmental provisions, boosting the resilience of the global trade order and better equipping it to tackle pressing environmental challenges.

This Element illustrates the diverse channels used to introduce environmental provisions into trade agreements, and demonstrates their potential for achieving environmental goals. We also discuss the prospects for multilateralization, showing how regime complexes enable innovative experiments and encourage flexible adaptation to changing environments. Rather than being seen as a waste of time and resources, false hopes, ineffective solutions, and diplomatic deadends should be viewed as part of a process that ultimately enhances governance at higher levels.

Contributions to Scholarship

Firstly, our work adds to the existing literature on interlinkages by providing a comprehensive and detailed analysis of the drivers and effects of the interplay between trade and environmental governance. Our analysis offers a nuanced understanding of the role of trade governance in environmental protection and governance, moving beyond the concepts of synergies and conflicts to highlight the trade-offs between SDGs. This enables us to address the important issue of policy coherence, in which the concept of trade-offs plays a central role.

Secondly, our research focuses on the role of trade agreements in environmental governance, with a particular emphasis on a broad range of PTAs. While there is existing research on trade-environment interlinkages within the WTO and select PTAs such as NAFTA, our work significantly contributes to understanding the drivers and impacts of these interlinkages across a larger sample of PTAs.

Thirdly, our research contributes to the literature on the trade regime complex and the benefits and drawbacks associated with such a structure. While regime complexes can lead to issues such as regime shifting and forum shopping, our analysis shows that the complex interplay between multiple institutions can enhance adaptability and resilience in global governance. Thus, our Element adds to the ongoing debate on whether and how regime complexes can be viewed as promoting normative advancements in global governance.

Future Research

This Element provides valuable insights into the interplay between trade and environmental governance, laying the groundwork for several avenues of future research.

Firstly, while environmental provisions in trade agreements can create synergies between economic and environmental sustainability, it is crucial to consider the social dimension of sustainable development. Future research should focus on strengthening public participation and stakeholder consultations to ensure that the social dimension is not neglected. The US-Peru agreement, which triggered social unrest because of inadequate consultation with stakeholders, is a useful reminder that greater integration of trade liberalization and environmental protection should not come at the cost of social inequality and instability (Jinnah & Morin, 2020).

Secondly, as global value chains (GVCs) play a significant role in economic development, it would be worthwhile to investigate the impact of environmental provisions in PTAs on upgrading GVCs. Previous studies suggest that environmental standards can facilitate such upgrades (Kummritz et al., 2017). However, more research is needed to explore how and to what extent this occurs.

Third, future research can expand on the co-evolution of trade and environmental governance systems. Studies can look simultaneously at the environmental content of trade agreements and the trade content of environmental agreements (on the latter, see Morin et al., 2023). It would be worthwhile to investigate how and why specific provisions move across regime complexes and adapt in the process.

Lastly, governance at the trade-environment interface is by no means a panacea. The underlying challenges, including problematic consumption patterns and power asymmetries, must be addressed with caution. Although it is not possible to address all practical problems in the short term, future research can offer guidance on how to navigate these challenges.

Policy Recommendations

Numerous decision-makers aim to develop mutually supportive policies (interviews with officials from Chile and New Zealand, 2017). To achieve this, decision-makers can make smart choices about treaty design and implement complementary measures to maximize win-win options. This Element provides key policy recommendations to guide the governance of the trade and environment interplay:

1. **Do no harm.** Several trade commitments can lead to adverse environmental consequences. Trade negotiators should include environmental exceptions in all chapters of any trade agreement, including in chapters related to foreign investment, and should protect states' capacity to regulate the environment.

2. **Focus on win-win solutions and manage trade-offs:** Future PTAs should focus on issues such as limiting fossil fuel subsidies, promoting trade in environmental goods and services, and greater access to patented environmental technologies that generate synergies between trade and the environment. Trade negotiators should also offer trade concessions to developing countries to counterbalance the potential trade-limiting impacts of certain environmental provisions.

3. **Promote participation of non-state actors:** There is a need to boost cooperation with civil society, from shaping to monitoring trade agreements. For example, in the EU, there should be a focus on reinstating the expert group on free trade agreements and strengthening domestic advisory groups. More generally, trade negotiators should make good use of environmental provisions that require the participation of NGOs or citizens in the adoption of environmental measures or during the implementation of PTAs.

4. **Boost capacity-building and assistance:** Decision-makers in high-income countries should focus on assistance for demand-driven capacity-building on environmental issues. Future PTAs should provide more precise commitments on environmental aid, with specific targets, amounts, and time frames. Policy-makers in high-income countries should also offer assistance to developing countries for implementing the environmental provisions in their PTAs.

5. **Improve impact assessment, data, and knowledge diffusion:** Impact assessments should be used more effectively. *Ex ante* assessments are highly uncertain and imprecise. Instead, policymakers should conduct regular *ex post* environmental assessments of agreements every five or ten years. This provides better learning opportunities, even in cases where measures are

unsuccessful or disappointing. Sharing knowledge and ensuring transparency can help to promote learning and diffuse good practices. Interactive visualization tools such as TREND Analytics (www.TRENDanalytics.info) can help make data on environmental provisions more easily accessible to trade negotiators, environmental NGOs, the private sector, or the wider public.

6. **Foster compliance and enforcement:** Concrete actions are required to advance and ensure that existing PTAs are effectively implemented and enforced. For example, in the EU, the Chief Trade Enforcement Officer should consolidate mechanisms for implementing and enforcing EU agreements, including their Trade and Sustainable Development chapters. Future PTAs should also specify sources of funding for implementing cooperative activities. With a view to enforcement, a hard sanction-based approach and softer cooperative approach can exist side-by-side within a given PTA. The two approaches are complementary when it comes to making major improvements to compliance.

7. **Make effective use of the trade-environment interface in the WTO:** The Trade and Environmental Sustainability Structured Discussions (TESSD) should continue to strike a balance between ambition and inclusiveness. Regular exchanges among trade negotiators can provide a basis for mutually beneficial exchanges that can help pave the way for multilateral progress on trade and the environment (e.g., in the context of the Forum on Trade, Environment and the SDGs (TESS) or during the WTO Public Forum).

8. **Focus on trade, climate change, and development:** Given the urgency of the climate crisis, trade and climate change should be a priority. A Trade Ministers' Coalition for Cooperation on Climate Action could strengthen international dialogue and coordinate strategies, options, and best practices for aligning climate and trade policies as well as development (Deere Birkbeck, 2021). In the context of PTAs, there should be focus on developing substantive and procedural options for climate-friendly trade agreements. Restrictions on fossil fuel subsidies, references to climate finance, the diffusion of climate-related technologies, emissions related to international freight, and broad exceptions to safeguard regulatory space for domestic climate regulation should be among the priorities (see also Brandi et al., forthcoming).

Overall, this Element provides practical inspiration to shape the global governance architecture in pursuit of the global common good, enriching our understanding of the interplay between global trade governance and global environmental governance. Recent developments, such as TESSD activities at the WTO and the planned Agreement on Climate Change, Trade, and Sustainability, offer hope. Interesting new trade-related endeavours are emerging beyond the framework of trade agreements, as illustrated by the growing number of countries using supply chain-based approaches to promote sustainability goals around the world (Schleifer et al., 2022). At the same time, more efforts are needed to promote synergies between international trade and environmental protection as well as the broader objective of sustainable development.

Acronyms and Abbreviations

AfCFTA	African Continental Free Trade Area
ASEAN	Association of Southeast Asian Nations
CAFTA	Central America Free Trade Agreement
CBAM	Carbon Border Adjustment Measure
CEPA	Comprehensive Economic Partnership Agreement
CITES	Convention on International Trade in Endangered Species of Wild Fauna and Flora
COMESA	Common Market for Eastern and Southern Africa
CPTTP	Comprehensive and Progressive Agreement for Trans-Pacific Partnership
DAG	Domestic Advisory Group
DG	Directorate Generals
DSM	Dispute Settlement Mechanisms
EGA	Environmental Goods Agreement
EPI	Environmental Protection Index
ESG	Earth System Governance
EU	European Union
FAST	Friends for Advancing Sustainable Trade (FAST)
FDI	Foreign Direct Investment
GATT	General Agreement on Tariffs and Trade
GDP	gross domestic product
GVC	Global Value Chains
ISPO	Indonesian Sustainable Palm Oil
MEA	Multilateral Environmental Agreements
NAFTA	North American Free Trade Agreement
NGO	non-governmental organization
PTA	preferential trade agreement
RCEP	Regional Comprehensive Economic Partnership (RCEP)
RSPO	Roundtable on Sustainable Palm Oil
SDG	Sustainable Development Goals
TESSD	Trade and Environmental Sustainability Structured Discussions
TPP	Trans-Pacific Partnership
TREND	Trade and Environment Database
TSD	Trade and Sustainable Development

UN	United Nations
UNFCCC	United Nations Framework Convention on Climate Change
US	United States of America
WHO	World Health Organization
WTO	World Trade Organization

Annex

List of Interviews

Year	Interviewee
2017	US negotiator for NAFTA
2017	Trade official, New Zealand
2017	Trade negotiator, Chile
2017	Trade negotiator, Switzerland
2021	European Commission, Trade
2021	Trade official, Germany
2021	Trade expert, UK
2021	European Commission, International Partnerships
2021	European Commission, International Partnerships

References

Abbott, K. W. (2012). The transnational regime complex for climate change. *Environment and Planning: Government and Policy, 30*(4), 571–90. https://doi.org/10.1068/c11127.

Abbott, K. W. (2014). Strengthening the transnational regime complex for climate change. *Transnational Environmental Law, 3*(1), 57–88.

Abman, R., & Lundberg, C. (2020). Does free trade increase deforestation? The effects of regional trade agreements. *Journal of the Association of Environmental and Resource Economists, 7*(1), 35–72.

Abman, R., Lundberg, C., & Ruta, M. (2021). *The Effectiveness of Environmental Provisions in Regional Trade Agreements.* Policy Research Working Paper 9601. World Bank.

Aggarwal, V. K. (2013). US free trade agreements and linkages. *International Negotiation, 18*(1), 89–110.

Allee, T., & Elsig, M. (2016). Why do some international institutions contain strong dispute settlement provisions? New evidence from preferential trade agreements. *The Review of International Organizations, 11*(1), 89–120.

Allee, T., & Elsig, M. (2019). Are the contents of international treaties copied and pasted? Evidence from preferential trade agreements. *International Studies Quarterly, 63*(3), 603–13. https://doi.org/10.1093/isq/sqz029.

Alschner, W., Pauwelyn, J., & Puig, S. (2017). The data-driven future of international economic law. *Journal of International Economic Law, 20*(2), 217–31.

Alter, K. J., & Meunier, S. (2009). The politics of international regime complexity. *Perspectives on Politics, 7*(1), 13–24. https://doi.org/10.1017/S1537592709090033.

Alter, K. J., & Raustiala, K. (2018). The rise of international regime complexity. *Annual Review of Law and Social Science, 14*, 329–49.

Association Agreement between the European Union and the European Atomic Energy Community and their Member States, of the one part, and Georgia, of the other part, European Union-Georgia, August 30, 2014, EUR-Lex.

Auld, G., Renckens, S., & Cashore, B. (2015). Transnational private governance between the logics of empowerment and control. *Regulation & Governance, 9*(2), 108–124.

Baccini, L. (2019). The economics and politics of preferential trade agreements. *Annual Review of Political Science, 22*, 75–92. https://doi.org/10.1146/annurev-polisci-050317-070708.

Baccini, L., & Dür, A. (2015). Investment discrimination and the proliferation of preferential trade agreements. *Journal of Conflict Resolution, 59*(4), 617–44. https://doi.org/10.1177/0022002713516844.

Baccini, L., & Urpelainen, J. (2012). Strategic side payments: Preferential trading agreements, economic reform, and foreign aid. *The Journal of Politics, 74*(4), 932-949.

Baccini, L., & Urpelainen, J. (2014). Before ratification: Understanding the timing of international treaty effects on domestic policies. *International Studies Quarterly, 58*(1), 29–43.

Baghdadi, L., Martinez–Zarzoso, I., & Zitouna, H. (2013). Are RTA agreements with environmental provisions reducing emissions. *Journal of International Economics, 90*(2), 378–90.

Baier, S. L., & Bergstrand, J. H. (2007). Do free trade agreements actually increase members' international trade? *Journal of International Economics, 71*(1), 72–95.

Baier, S. L., Bergstrand, J. H., & Feng, M. (2014). Economic integration agreements and the margins of international trade. *Journal of International Economics, 93*(2), 339–50. https://doi.org/10.1016/j.jinteco.2014.03.005.

Baker, P. R. (2021). *Handbook on Negotiating Sustainable Development Provisions in Preferential Trade Agreements*. United Nations.

Baldwin, R. E., (2010). Understanding the GATT's wins and the WTO's woes. Policy Insight, 49, 1–12.

Baldwin, R. (2014). WTO 2.0: Governance of the 21st century trade. *Review of International Organization, 9*(2), 261–83. https://doi.org/10.1007/s11558-014-9186-4.

Baldwin, R., & Jaimovich, D. (2012). Are free trade agreements contagious? *Journal of International Economics, 88*(1), 1–16. https://doi.org/10.1016/j.jinteco.2012.03.009.

Baldwin, R., & Low, P., eds. (2009). *Multilateralizing Regionalism: Challenges for the Global Trading System*. Cambridge University Press. https://doi.org/10.1017/CBO9781139162111.

Bastiaens, I., & Postnikov, E. (2017). Greening up: The effects of environmental standards in EU and US trade agreements. *Environmental Politics, 26*(5), 847–69. https://doi.org/10.1080/09644016.2017.1338213.

Bastiaens, I., & Postnikov, E. (2020). Social standards in trade agreements and free trade preferences: An empirical investigation. *The Review of International Organizations, 15*, 793–816.

Bayramoglu, B., Gozlan, E., Nedoncelle, C., & Tarabbia, T. (2023). *Trade Agreements and Sustainable Fisheries*. Working Papers Hal-04101044. HAL.

Bechtel, M. M., Bernauer, T., & Meyer, R. (2012). The green side of protectionism: Environmental concerns and three facets of trade policy preferences. *Review of International Political Economy*, *19*(5), 837–66.

Bellmann, C., & Tipping, A. V. (2015). The role of trade and trade policy in advancing the 2030 Development Agenda. *International Development Policy*, *6*(2), 1–27.

Benson, E., Janardhan, S., & Reinsch, W. A. (2022). *Multilateral Trade Arrangements and Climate Provisions: Strengthening Standards in Sectoral Agreements*. Center for Strategic & International Studies.

Berger, A., Blümer, D., Brandi, C., & Chi, M. (2020). Towards greening trade? Environmental provisions in emerging markets' preferential trade agreements. In A. Negi, P.P. Jorge Antonio, & J. Blankenbach, eds. (2020). *Sustainability Standards and Global Governance*. Springer, pp. 61–81.

Berger, A., Brandi, C., Bruhn, D., & Morin, J.-F. (2017). *TREND Analytics: Environmental Provisions in Preferential Trade Agreements*. German Development Institute/Deutsches Institut für Entwicklungspolitik (DIE). https://doi.org/10.23661/trendanalytics_2017_1.0.

Berger, A., Brandi, C., Morin, J.-F., & Schwab, J. (2020). The trade effects of environmental provisions in preferential trade agreements. In Beverelli, C., Kurtz, J. & Raess, D., eds., *International Trade, Investment, and the Sustainable Development Goals*. Cambridge University Press, pp. 111–39. https://doi.org/10.1017/9781108881364.006.

Bernauer, T., & Nguyen, Q. (2015). Free trade and/or environmental protection? *Global Environmental Politics*, *15*(4), 105–29.

Betsill, M., Dubash, N. K., Paterson, M., et al. (2015). Building productive links between the UNFCCC and the broader global climate governance landscape. *Global Environmental Politics*, *15*(2), 1–10.

Beverelli, C., Kurtz, J., & Raess, D. (2020). *International Trade, Investment, and the Sustainable Development Goals*. Cambridge University Press. https://doi.org/10.1017/9781108881364.

Bhagwati, J. (1993). Trade and the environment: The false conflict? *Trade and the Environment: Law, Economics and Policy*, *1*, 159–223.

Bhagwati, J. (1995). *US Trade Policy: The Infatuation with FTAs*. Department of Economics, Columbia University: Discussion Paper Series No. 726. https://doi.org/10.7916/D8CN7BFM.

Bhagwati, J. (2008). *Termites in the Trading System: How Preferential Agreements Undermine Free Trade*. Oxford University Press.

Bhagwati, J. N., & Hudec, R. E., eds. (1996). *Fair Trade and Harmonization: Prerequisites for Free Trade?* MIT Press.

Biermann, F. (2014). *Earth System Governance: World Politics in the Anthropocene*. MIT Press. https://doi.org/10.1017/S153759271500345X.

Biermann, F., & Kim, R. E. (2020). Architectures of earth system governance: Setting the stage. In F. Biermann & R. E. Kim, eds., *Architectures of Earth System Governance: Institutional Complexity and Structural Transformation*. Cambridge University Press.

Biermann, F., Betsill, M. M., Gupta, J., et al. (2009a). Earth System Governance Project: People, Places, and the Planet: Science and Implementation Plan of the Earth System Governance Project. Earth System Governance Project. Earth System Governance Project Report No. 1, IHDP report No. 20. IDHP.

Biermann, F., Pattberg, P., Van Asselt, H., & Zelli, F. (2009b). The fragmentation of global governance architectures: A framework for analysis. *Global Environmental Politics*, *9*(4), 14–40. https://doi.org/10.1162/glep.2009.9.4.14.

Birkbeck, C. D. (2021). *Priorities for the Climate-Trade Agenda: How a Trade Ministers' Coalition for Cooperation on Climate Action Could Help*. The Royal Institute of International Affairs.

Blatter, J., Portmann, L., & Rausis, F. (2022). Theorizing policy diffusion: from a patchy set of mechanisms to a paradigmatic typology. *Journal of European Public Policy*, *29*(6), 805–825.

Blümer, D., Morin, J.-F., Brandi, C., & Berger, A. (2020). Environmental provisions in trade agreements: Defending regulatory space or pursuing offensive interests? *Environmental Politics*, *29*(5), 866–89.

Bondi, A., & Hoekman, B. (2022). *Non-Trade Objectives and EU External Policy: Survey Responses on RESPECT Research Findings*. Robert Schuman Centre for Advance Studies.

Brandi, C. (2017). The trade regime complex and Megaregionals: An exploration from the perspective of international domination. *Global Justice: Theory Practice Rhetoric*, *10*(1), 24–42. https://doi.org/10.21248/gjn.10.1.109.

Brandi, C., Blümer, D., & Morin, J.-F. (2019). When do international treaties matter for domestic environmental legislation? *Global Environmental Politics*, *19*(4), 14–44.

Brandi, C., Holzer, K., Morin, J.-F., & van Asselt, H. (forthcoming). Taking climate change seriously in the design of trade agreements. In M. Elsig & R. Palanco, eds., *The Concept Design of 21 Century Trade Agreements*. Cambridge University Press.

Brandi, C., Morin, J.-F., & Stender, F. (2022). Do greener trade agreements call for side-payments? *The Journal of Environment & Development*, *31*(2), 111–38. https://doi.org/10.1177/10704965221076070.

Brandi, C., Schwab, J., Berger, A., & Morin, J.-F. (2020). Do environmental provisions in trade agreements make exports from developing countries greener? *World Development*, *129*, 104899.

Brock, D. (2022). *Improving Forest Governance in Relation to Palm Oil*. Fern.

Bronckers, M., & Gruni, G. (2021). Retooling the sustainability standards in EU Free Trade Agreements. *Journal of International Economic Law*, *24*(1), 25–51.

Burch, S., Gupta, A., Inoue, C. Y., et al. (2019). New directions in earth system governance research. *Earth System Governance*, *1*, 100006. https://doi.org/10.1016/j.esg.2019.100006.

Cao, X. (2010). Networks as channels of policy diffusion: Explaining worldwide changes in capital taxation, 1998–2006. *International Studies Quarterly*, *54*(3), 823–54.

CARICOM (2001). Revised Treaty of Chaguaramas Establishing the Caribbean Community Including the CARICOM Single Market and Economy. CARICOM, 2001, Caribbean Community (CARICOM) Secretariat.

Cima, E. (2018). Promoting renewable energy through FTAs? The legal implications of a new generation of trade agreements. *Journal of World Trade*, *52*(4), 663–695.

Charnovitz, S. (2007). The WTO's environmental progress. *Journal of International Economic Law*, *10*(3), 685–706. https://doi.org/10.1093/jiel/jgm027.

Cherniwchan, J. (2017). Trade liberalization and the environment: Evidence from NAFTA and US manufacturing. *Journal of International Economics*, *105*, 130–49. https://doi.org/10.1016/j.jinteco.2017.01.005.

Cherniwchan, J., & Taylor, M. S. (2022). *International Trade and the Environment: Three Remaining Empirical Challenges*. NBER Working Paper w30020.

Cherniwchan, J., Copeland, B. R., & Taylor, M. S. (2017). Trade and the environment: New methods, measurements, and results. *Annual Review of Economics*, *9*, 59–85.

Cohen, M. A., & Tubb, A. (2018). The impact of environmental regulation on firm and country competitiveness: A meta-analysis of the porter hypothesis. *Journal of the Association of Environmental and Resource Economists*, *5*(2), 371–99. https://doi.org/10.1086/695613.

Colgan, J. D., Green, J.-F., & Hale, T. N. (2021). Asset revaluation and the existential politics of climate change. *International Organization*, *75*(2), 586–610.

Conca, K. (2000). The WTO and the undermining of global environmental governance. *Review of International Political Economy*, *7*(3), 484–94.

Congress Research Service. (2008). *Trade Capacity Building: Foreign Assistance for Trade and Development*. The Library of Congress.

Convention on International Trade in Endangered Species of Wild Fauna and Flora (CITES), IUCN, March 3, 1973, CITES

Convention on Biological Diversity (CBD), UN, 5 June, 1992, CBD

Copeland, B. R., & Taylor, M. S. (1994). North-South trade and the environment. *The Quarterly Journal of Economics*, *109*(3), 755–87. https://doi.org/10.2307/2118421.

Daly, H. E. (1993). The perils of free trade. *Scientific American*, *269*(5), 50–7. www.jstor.org/stable/24941683.

De Búrca, G. D., Keohane, R. O., & Sabel, C. (2014). Global experimentalist governance. *British Journal of Political Science*, *44*(3), 477–86.

Dent, C. M. (2021). Trade, climate and energy: A new study on climate action through free trade agreements. *Energies*, *14*(14), 1–30. https://doi.org/10.3390/en14144363.

Di Ubaldo, M., & Gasiorek, M. (2022). Non-trade provisions in trade agreements and FDI. *European Journal of Political Economy*, *75*, 102208.

Downs, G. W., Rocke, D. M., & Barsoom, P. N. (1996). Is the good news about compliance good news about cooperation? *International organization*, *50*(3), 379-406.

Draper, P., Khumalo, N., & Tigere, F. (2017). *Sustainability Provisions in Regional Trade Agreements: Can They Be Multilateralised?* International Centre for Trade and Sustainable Development. https://doi.org/10.13140/RG.2.2.10268.44164.

Duit, A., Galaz, V., Eckerberg, K., & Ebbesson, J. (2020). Governance, complexity, and resilience. *Global Environmental Change*, *20*, 363–8.

Dür, A., Baccini, L., & Elsig, M. (2014). The design of international trade agreements: Introducing a new dataset. *The Review of International Organizations*, *9*(3), 353–75. https://doi.org/10.1007/s11558-013-9179-8.

Dür, A., Huber, R. A., Mateo, G., & Spilker, G. (2022). Interest group preferences towards trade agreements: Institutional design matters. *Interest Groups & Advocacy*, *12*, 48–72.

Durán, G. M. (2020). Sustainable development chapters in EU free trade agreements: Emerging compliance issues. *Common Market Law Review*, *57*(4), 1031–68.

Eckersley, R. (2004). The big chill: The WTO and multilateral environmental agreements. *Global Environmental Politics*, *4*(2), 24–50. https://doi.org/10.1162/152638004323074183.

Elkins, Z., & Simmons, B. (2005). On waves, clusters, and diffusion: A conceptual framework. *The Annals of the American Academy of Political and Social Science, 598*(1), 33–51. https://doi.org/10.1177/000271620 4272516.

Esty, D. C. (1994). *Greening the GATT: Trade, Environment, and the Future*. Peterson Institute.

European Commission (2015). *Trade for All: Towards a More Responsible Trade and Investment Policy*.

European Commission (2017). *FTA Implementation Report*. COM/2017/0654 final.

European Commission (2018). *Feedback and Way Forward on Improving the Implementation and Enforcement of Trade and Sustainable Development Chapters in EU Free Trade Agreements*.

Faude, B. (2020). Breaking gridlock: How path dependent layering enhances resilience in global trade governance. *Global Policy, 11*(4), 448–57. https://doi.org/10.1111/1758-5899.12822.

Faude, B., & Große-Kreul, F. (2020). Let's justify! How regime complexes enhance the normative legitimacy of global governance. *International Studies Quarterly, 64*(2), 431–9. https://doi.org/10.1093/isq/sqaa024.

Finnemore, M., & Sikkink, K. (1998). International norm dynamics and political change. *International Organization, 52*(4), 887–917.

Francois, J., Hoekman, B., Manchin, M., & Santi, F. (2023). *Pursuing Environmental and Social Objectives through Trade Agreements*. Policy Research Paper 10323. World Bank.

Gagné, G., & Morin, J.-F. (2006). The evolving American policy on investment protection: Evidence from recent FTAs and the 2004 model BIT. *Journal of International Economic Law, 9*(2), 357–82.

Gallagher, K. (2004). *Free Trade and the Environment: Mexico, NAFTA, and Beyond*. Stanford University Press.

Gallagher, K., ed. (2005). *Putting Development First: The Importance of Policy Space in the WTO and IFIs*. Zed Books.

Gamso, J. (2017). Trade partnerships and environmental performance in developing countries. *The Journal of Environment & Development, 26*(4), 375–99. https://doi.org/10.1177/1070496517729727.

Gamso, J., & Postnikov, E. (2022). Leveling-up: Explaining the depth of South-South trade agreements. *Review of International Political Economy, 29*(5), 1601–24.

Gehring, T., & Faude, B. (2013). The dynamics of regime complexes: Microfoundations and systemic effects. *Global Governance: A Review of Multilateralism and International Organizations, 19*(1), 119–30. https://doi.org/10.1163/19426720-01901010.

Gehring, T., & Faude, B. (2014). A theory of emerging order within institutional complexes: How competition among regulatory international institutions leads to institutional adaptation and division of labor. *The Review of International Organizations*, *9*, 471–98.

George, C. (2014). *Environment and Regional Trade Agreements*. OECD Trade and Environment, Working Paper 2014/02. https://doi.org/10.1787/18166881.

Gilardi, F. (2012). Transnational diffusion: Norms, ideas, and policies. In W. Carlsnaes, T. Risse, & B. Simmons, eds., *Handbook of International Relations*. Sage, pp. 453–77.

Gilardi, F., & Wasserfallen, F. (2019). The politics of policy diffusion. *European Journal of Political Research*, *58*(4), 1245–56. https://doi.org/10.1111/1475-6765.12326.

Gómez-Mera, L., Morin, J.-F., & Van de Graaf, T. (2020). Regime complexes. In F. Biermann & R. E. Kim Edu, eds., *Architectures of Earth System Governance: Institutional Complexity and Structural Transformation*. Cambridge University Press, pp. 137–57.

Government Accountability Office (2005). *Foreign Assistance: U.S. Trade Capacity Building Extensive, but Its Effectiveness Has Yet to Be Evaluated*. GAO Report Number GAO-05-150. www.gao.gov/assets/gao-05-150.pdf.

Grossman, G. M., & Krueger, A. B. (1991). *Environmental Impacts of a North American Free Trade Agreement*. NBER Working Paper 3914.

Hale, T. (2020). Catalytic cooperation. *Global Environmental Politics*, *20*(4), 73–98.

Hale, T., Held, D., & Young, K. (2013). *Gridlock: Why Global Cooperation Is Failing When We Need It Most*. Polity Press.

Harrison, J., Barbu, M., Campling, L., Richardson, B., & Smith, A. (2019). Governing labour standards through free trade agreements: Limits of the European Union's trade and sustainable development chapters. *JCMS: Journal of common market studies*, *57*(2), 260–77.

Hickmann, T., van Asselt, H., Oberthür, S., et al. (2020). Institutional interlinkages. In F. Biermann & R. E. Kim, eds., In *Architectures of Earth System Governance: Institutional Complexity and Structural Transformation*. Cambridge University Press, 119–36.

Hoang, N. T., & Kanemoto, K. (2021). Mapping the deforestation footprint of nations reveals growing threat to tropical forests. *Nature Ecology & Evolution*, *5*(6), 845–53.

Hoekman, B. (2014). Sustaining multilateral trade cooperation in a multipolar world economy. *The Review of International Organizations*, *9*(2), 241–60.

Hoekman, B., & Sabel, C. (2019). Open plurilateral agreements, international regulatory cooperation and the WTO. *Global Policy*, *10*(3), 297–312.

Hoekman, B., Santi, F., & Shingal, A. (2023). Trade effects of non-economic provisions in trade agreements. *Economics Letters*, *226*, 111081.

Hollway, J., Morin, J.-F., & Pauwelyn, J. (2020). Structural conditions for novelty: The introduction of new environmental clauses to the trade regime complex. *International Environmental Agreements: Politics, Law and Economics*, *20*(1), 61–83.

Hong, C., Zhao, H., Qin, Y., et al. (2022). Land-use emissions embodied in international trade. *Science*, *376*(6593), 597–603.

Horn, H., Mavroidis, P. C., & Sapir, A. (2010). Beyond the WTO? An anatomy of EU and US preferential trade agreements. *The World Economy*, *33*(11), 1565–88. https://doi.org/10.1111/j.1467-9701.2010.01273.x.

Hradilova, K., & Svoboda, O. (2018). Sustainable development chapters in the EU free trade agreements: Searching for effectiveness. *Journal of World Trade*, *52*(6), 1019–42. https://doi.org/10.54648/TRAD2018044.

Hufbauer, G. C., Esty, D. C., Orejas, D., Schott, J. J., & Rubio, L. (2000). *NAFTA and the Environment: Seven Years Later*. Peterson Institute.

Jetschke, A., & Lenz, T. (2013). Does regionalism diffuse? A new research agenda for the study of regional organizations. *Journal of European Public Policy*, *20*(4), 626–37.

Jinnah, S. (2010). Overlap management in the World Trade Organization: Secretariat influence on trade-environment politics. *Global Environmental Politics*, *10*(2), 54–79. https://doi.org/10.1162/glep.2010.10.2.54.

Jinnah, S. (2011). Strategic linkages: The evolving role of trade agreements in global environmental governance. *The Journal of Environment & Development*, *20*(2), 191–215. https://doi.org/10.1177/1070496511405152.

Jinnah, S. (2014). *Post-treaty Politics: Secretariat Influence in Global Environmental Governance*. MIT Press. https://doi.org/10.1017/S20471025 1700005X.

Jinnah, S., & Lindsay, A. (2016). Diffusion through issue linkage: Environmental norms in US trade agreements. *Global Environmental Politics*, *16*(3), 41–61.

Jinnah, S., & Morgera, E. (2013). Environmental provisions in American and EU free trade agreements: A preliminary comparison and research agenda. *Review of European, Comparative & International Environmental Law*, *22*(3), 324–39. https://doi.org/10.1111/reel.12042.

Jinnah, S., & Morin, J.-F. (2020). *Greening through Trade: How American Trade Policy Is Linked to Environmental Protection Abroad*. MIT Press.

Johnson, T. (2015). Information revelation and structural supremacy: The World Trade Organization's incorporation of environmental policy. *The Review of International Organizations*, *10*(2), 207–29. https://doi.org/10.1007/s11558-015-9215-y.

Keohane, R., & Victor, D. (2009). *The Regime Complex for Climate Change*. Harvard Project on International Climate Agreements.

Keohane, R., & Victor, D. (2011). The regime complex for climate change. *Perspectives on Politics*, *9*(1), 7–23. www.jstor.org/stable/41622723.

Kettunen, M., et al. (2021). *Environmental Credentials of EU Trade Policy*. Institute for European Environmental Policy.

Kolcava, D., Nguyen, Q., & Bernauer, T. (2019). Does trade liberalization lead to environmental burden shifting in the global economy? *Ecological Economics*, *163*, 98–112.

Krugman, P. R. (1997). *Development, Geography, and Economic Theory*. MIT Press.

Kummritz, V., Taglioni, D., & Winkler, D. E. (2017). *Economic Upgrading through Global Value Chain Participation: Which Policies Increase the Value Added Gains?* Policy Research Working Paper 8007. World Bank.

Laurens, N., & Morin, J.-F. (2019). Negotiating environmental protection in trade agreements: A regime shift or a tactical linkage? *International Environmental Agreements: Politics, Law and Economics*, *19*(6), 533–56.

Lechner, L. (2016). The domestic battle over the design of non-trade issues in preferential trade agreements. *Review of International Political Economy*, *23*(5), 840–71. https://doi.org/10.1080/09692290.2016.1231130.

Lechner, L. (2018). Good for some, bad for others: US investors and non-trade issues in preferential trade agreements. *The Review of International Organizations*, *13*(2), 163–87. https://doi.org/10.1007/s11558-018-9299-2.

Lechner, L., & Spilker, G. (2021). Taking it seriously: Commitments to the environment in South-South preferential trade agreements. *Environmental Politics*, *31*(6), 1–23. https://doi.org/10.1080/09644016.2021.1975399.

Marshall, M. G., Gurr, T. R., & Jaggers, K. (2020). Political regime characteristics and transitions, 1800–2018: Dataset users' manual. *Polity IV Project*. www.systemicpeace.org/polityproject.html.

Martínez-Zarzoso, I., & Oueslati, W. (2018). Do deep and comprehensive regional trade agreements help in reducing air pollution? *International Environmental Agreements: Politics, Law and Economics*, *18*(6), 743–77. https://doi.org/10.1007/s10784-018-9414-0.

Mealy, P., & Teytelboym, A. (2020). Economic complexity and the green economy. *Research Policy*, *51*(8). https://doi.org/10.1016/j.respol.2020.103948.

Meunier, S., & Morin, J.-F. (2015). No agreement is an island: Negotiating TTIP in a dense regime complex. In J.-F. Morin, T. Novotná, F. Ponjaert, & M. Tel, eds., *The Politics of Transatlantic Trade Negotiations*. Routledge, pp. 173–86.

Meunier, S., & Nicolaïdis, K. (2006). The European Union as a conflicted trade power. *Journal of European Public Policy*, *13*(6), 906–25.

Meyer, T. (2017). Explaining energy disputes at the World Trade Organization. *International Environmental Agreements: Politics, Law and Economics*, *17* (3), 391–410. https://doi.org/10.1007/s10784-017-9356-y.

Milewicz, K., Hollway, J., Peacock, C., & Snidal, D. (2018). Beyond trade: The expanding scope of the nontrade agenda in trade agreements. *Journal of Conflict Resolution*, *62*(4), 743-773. https://doi.org/10.1177/0022002716 662687.

Mitchell, R. B. (2006). Problem structure, institutional design, and the relative effectiveness of international environmental agreements. *Global Environmental Politics*, *6*(3), 72–89. https://doi.org/10.1162/glep.2006 .6.3.72.

Morin, J.-F., & Bialais, C. (2018). Strengthening multilateral environmental governance through bilateral trade deals. *Centre for International Governments Innovation*, *123*, 1-8

Morin, J.-F., Blümer, D., Brandi, C., & Berger, A. (2019a). Kick-starting diffusion: Explaining the varying frequency of preferential trade agreements' environmental provisions by their initial conditions. *The World Economy*, *42* (9), 2602–28. https://doi.org/10.1111/twec.12822.

Morin, J.-F., Brandi, C., & Berger, A. (2019b). The multilateralization of PTAs' environmental clauses: Scenarios for the future. In M. Elsig, M. Hahn, & G. Spilker, eds., *The Shifting Landscape of Global Trade Governance: World Trade Forum*. pp. 207–32. Cambridge University Press. https://doi.org/ 10.1017/9781108757683.009.

Morin, J.-F, Brandi, C., & Schwab, J. (2023). Environmental agreements as clubs: Evidence from a new dataset of trade provisions. The Review of International Organizations, 1–30. https://doi.org/10.1007/s11558-023-09495-3.

Morin, J.-F., Chaudhuri, V., & Gauquelin, M. (2018a). *Do Trade Deals Encourage Environmental Cooperation?* Briefing Paper 8/2018. German Development Institute/Deutsches Institut für Entwicklungspolitik (DIE). https://doi.org/10.23661/bp8.2018.

Morin, J.-F., Dür, A., & Lechner, L. (2018b). Mapping the trade and environment nexus: Insights from a new data set. *Global Environmental Politics*, *18* (1), 122–39. https://doi.org/10.1162/GLEP_a_00447.

Morin, J.-F., & Gauquelin, M. (2016). *Trade Agreements as Vectors for the Nagoya Protocol's Implementation*. CIGI Paper 115.

Morin, J.-F., & Gauthier-Nadeau, R. (2017). *Environmental Gems in Trade Agreements: Little-known Clauses for Progressive Trade Agreements*. CIGI Papers 148.

Morin, J.-F., & Jinnah, S. (2018). The untapped potential of preferential trade agreements for climate governance. *Environmental Politics*, *27*(3), 541–65.

Morin, J.-F., Pauwelyn, J., & Hollway, J. (2017). The trade regime as a complex adaptive system: Exploration and exploitation of environmental norms in trade agreements. *Journal of International Economic Law*, *20*(2), 365–90.

Morin, J.-F., & Rochette, M. (2017). Transatlantic convergence of PTAs' environmental clauses. *Business and Politics*, *19*(4), 621–58.

Morse, J. C., & Keohane, R. O. (2014). Contested multilateralism. *The Review of International Organizations*, *9*(4), 385–412. https://doi.org/10.1007/s11558-014-9188-2.

Narlikar, A. (2003). *International Trade and Developing Countries: Bargaining Coalitions in the GATT & WTO*. Taylor & Francis.

Narlikar, A. (2010). New powers in the club: The challenges of global trade governance. *International Affairs*, *86*(3), 717–28. https://doi.org/10.1111/j.1468-2346.2010.00907.x.

Neumayer, E. (2004). The WTO and the environment: Its past record is better than critics believe, but the future outlook is bleak. *Global Environmental Politics*, *4*(3), 1–8. https://doi.org/10.1162/1526380041748083.

Oberthür, S., & Gehring, T. (2006a). Conceptual foundations of institutional interaction. In S. Oberthür & T. Gehring, eds., *Institutional Interaction in Global Environmental Governance: Synergy and Conflict among International and EU Policies*. MIT Press, 19–52. https://doi.org/10.7551/mitpress/3808.001.0001.

Oberthür, S., & Gehring, T., eds. (2006b). *Institutional Interaction in Global Environmental Governance: Synergy and Conflict among International and EU Policies*. MIT Press.

Oberthür, S., & Gehring, T. (2011). Institutional interaction: Ten years of scholarly development. In S. Oberthür & O. S. Stokke, eds., *Managing Institutional Complexity: Regime Interplay and Global Environmental Change*. MIT Press.

OECD (2019). *Policy Coherence for Sustainable Development 2019: Empowering People and Ensuring Inclusiveness and Equality*. Organisation for Economic Co-operation and Development.

Orsini, A., Morin, J.-F., & Young, O. (2013). Regime complexes: A buzz, a boom, or a boost for global governance? *Global Governance: A Review of Multilateralism and International Organizations*, *19*(1), 27–39.

Pattberg, P. (2010). Public-private partnerships in global climate governance. *WIREs Climate Change*, *1*(2), 279–87. https://doi.org/10.1002/wcc.38.

Pattberg, P., & Widerberg, O. (2016). Transnational multistakeholder partnerships for sustainable development: Conditions for success. *Ambio*, *45*, 42–51. https://doi.org/10.1007/s13280-015-0684-2.

Pattberg, P. H., & Zelli, F. (2016). Global environmental governance in the Anthropocene. Routledge.

Pauwelyn, J. (2014). At the edge of chaos? Foreign investment law as a complex adaptive system, how it emerged and how it can be reformed. *ICSID Review*, *29*(2), 372–418.

Pauwelyn, J., & Alschner, W. (2015). Forget about the WTO: The network of relations between Preferential Trade Agreements (PTAs) and 'Double PTAs'. In A. Dür & M. Elsig, eds., *Trade Operation: The Purpose, Design and Effects of Preferential Trade Agreements*. Cambridge University Press, pp. 497–532.

Peacock, C., Milewicz, K., & Snidal, D. (2019). Boilerplates in international trade agreements. *International Studies Quarterly*, *63*(4), 923–37.

Pendrill, F., Persson, U. M., Godar, J., et al. (2019). Agricultural and forestry trade drives large share of tropical deforestation emissions. *Global Environmental Change*, *56*, 1–10.

Poletti, A., & Sicurelli, D. (2016). The European Union, preferential trade agreements, and the international regulation of sustainable biofuels. *Journal of Common Market Studies*, *54*(2), 249–66.

Poletti, A., & Sicurelli, D. (2018). *The Political Economy of Normative Trade Power Europe*. Palgrave Macmillan.

Porter, M. E. (1991). Towards a dynamic theory of strategy. *Strategic Management Journal*, *12*(S2), 95–117. https://doi.org/10.1002/smj.4250121008.

Porter, M. E., & Van der Linde, C. (1995). Toward a new conception of the environment-competitiveness relationship. *Journal of Economic Perspectives*, *9*(4), 97–118. https://doi.org/10.1257/jep.9.4.97.

Postnikov, E. (2020). *Social Standards in EU and US Trade Agreements*. Routledge.

Poulsen, L. N. (2014). Bounded rationality and the diffusion of modern investment treaties. *International Studies Quarterly*, *58*(1), 1–14. https://doi.org/10.1111/isqu.12051.

Prakash, A., & Potoski, M. (2006). Racing to the bottom? Trade, environmental governance, and ISO 14001. *American Journal of Political Science*, *50*(2), 350–64.

Prakash, A., & Potoski, M. (2007). Investing up: FDI and the cross-country diffusion of ISO 14001 management systems. *International Studies Quarterly, 51*(3), 723–44.

Prakash, A., & Potoski, M. (2017). The EU effect: Does trade with the EU reduce CO_2 emissions in the developing world? *Environmental Politics, 26*(1), 27–48.

Pulkowski, D. (2014). *The Law and Politics of International Regime Conflict.* Oxford University Press.

Raustiala, K., & Victor, D. G. (2004). The regime complex for plant genetic resources. *International Organization, 58*(2), 277–309. www.jstor.org/stable/3877859.

Ricardo, D. (1817). On the Principles of Political Economy and Taxation.

Rickard, S. J. (2022). Interests, institutions, and the environment: An examination of fisheries subsidies. *International Studies Quarterly, 66*(2), 1–14.

Rojas-Romagosa, H. (2020). Trade agreements, non-trade provisions and bilateral foreign direct investment. *Great Insights Magazine*, June.

Sato, M. (2014). Embodied carbon in trade: A survey of the empirical literature. *Journal of Economic Surveys, 28*(5), 831–61.

Scott, J. (2015). The role of Southern intellectuals in contemporary trade governance. *New Political Economy, 20*(5), 633–652.

Schleifer, P., Brandi, C., Verma, R., Bissinger, K., & Fiorini, M. (2022). Voluntary standards and the SDGs: Mapping public-private complementarities for sustainable development. Earth System Governance, 14, 100153.

Shapiro, J. S. (2021). The environmental bias of trade policy. *The Quarterly Journal of Economics, 136*(2), 831–86.

Sieber-Gasser, C. (2021). The EFTA-Indonesia template for sustainable palm-oil. *Human Rights in Context*, 29 April. www.humanrightsincontext.be/post/the-efta-indonesia-template-for-sustainable-palm-oil-and-for-human-rights.

Simmons, B. A., Dobbin, F., & Garrett, G., eds. (2008). *The Global Diffusion of Markets and Democracy.* Cambridge University Press.

Simmons, B. A., & Elkins, Z. (2004). The globalization of liberalization: Policy diffusion in the international political economy. *American Political Science Review, 98*(1), 171–89.

Sprinz, D. F., & Vaahtoranta, T. (1994). The interest-based explanation of international environmental policy. *International Organization, 48*(1), 77–105.

Stokke, O. S. (2000). Managing straddling stocks: The interplay of global and regional regimes. *Ocean & Coastal Management, 43*(2–3), 205–34. https://doi.org/10.1016/S0964-5691(99)00071-X.

Stokke, O. S. (2001). *The Interplay of International Regimes: Putting Effectiveness Theory to Work.* Fridtjof Nansen Institute.

Susskind, L. E., & Ali, S. H. (2014). *Environmental Diplomacy: Negotiating More Effective Global Agreements*. Oxford University Press.

Trachtman, J. P. (2018). WTO trade and environment jurisprudence: Avoiding environmental catastrophe. *Harvard International Law Journal*, *58*(2), 1–38.

Tröster, R., & Hiete, M. (2018). Success of voluntary sustainability certification schemes: A comprehensive review. *Journal of Cleaner Production*, *196*, 1034–43.

United Nations Framework Convention on Climate Change (UNFCCC), UN, June 12,1992, UNFCCC

UNFCCC (2015). *Paris Agreement to the United Nations Framework Convention on Climate Change*, 12 December.

United Nations (2015). *Transforming Our World: The 2030 Agenda for Sustainable Development*. UN General Assembly, 21 October.

Van Asselt, H. (2014). *The Fragmentation of Global Climate Governance: Consequences and Management of Regime Interactions*. Edward Elgar.

Van Asselt, H., & Zelli, F. (2014). Connect the dots: Managing the fragmentation of global climate governance. *Environmental Economics and Policy Studies*, *16*, 137–55.

Vandeveer, S. D., & Dabelko, G. (2001). It's capacity, stupid: International assistance and national implementation. *Global Environmental Politics*, *1*(2), 18–29.

Velut, J. B., et al. (2022). Comparative analysis of TSD provisions for identification of best practices to support the TSD review. *LSE*.

Vignarelli, M. C. (2021). The European Commission trade policy review: The effectiveness of sustainable development chapters in EU FTAs. *European Papers: A Journal on Law and Integration*, *6*(1), 1–5.

Vogel, D. (1997). Trading up and governing across: transnational governance and environmental protection. *Journal of European public policy*, *4*(4), 556–571

Vogel, D. (2009). *Trading Up: Consumer and Environmental Regulation in a Global Economy*. Harvard University Press.

Wiedmann, T., & Lenzen, M. (2018). Environmental and social footprints of international trade. *Nature Geoscience*, *11*(5), 314–321.

Weyland, K. (2005). Theories of policy diffusion lessons from Latin American pension reform. *World Politics*, *57*(2), 262–95. https://doi.org/10.1353/wp.2005.0019.

Winters, L. A., & Martuscelli, A. (2014). Trade liberalization and poverty: What have we learned in a decade? *Annual Review Resource Economics*, *6*(1), 493–512.

WTO (2020). Communication on Trade and Environmental Sustainability, WTO, November 17, 2020, WTO.

WTO (2021). Trade and Environmental Sustainability Structured Discussions, WTO, December 15, 2021, WTO

Yildirim, A., Basedow, R., Fiorini, M., & Hoekman, B. (2021). EU trade and non-trade objectives: New survey evidence on policy design and effectiveness. *Journal of Common Market Studies*, *59*(3), 556–68. https://doi.org/10.1111/jcms.13100.

Young, M. A. (2009). Fragmentation or interaction: The WTO, fisheries subsidies, and international law. *World Trade Review*, *8*(4), 477–515.

Young, O. R. (1996). Institutional linkages in international society: Polar perspectives. *Global Governance*, *2*(1), 1–24. www.jstor.org/stable/27800125.

Young, O. R. (2001). Inferences and indices: Evaluating the effectiveness of international environmental regimes. *Global Environmental Politics*, *1*(1), 99–121. https://doi.org/10.1162/152638001570651.

Young, O. R. (2012). Arctic tipping points: Governance in turbulent times. *Ambio*, *41*(1), 75–84. https://doi.org/10.1007/s13280-011-0227-4.

Young, O. R., & Gasser, L. (2002). *The Institutional Dimensions of Environmental Change: Fit, Interplay, and Scale*. MIT press. https://doi.org/10.7551/mitpress/3807.001.0001.

Zelli, F., Gupta, A., & Van Asselt, H. (2013). Institutional interactions at the crossroads of trade and environment: The dominance of liberal environmentalism? *Global Governance*, *19*(1), 105–18.

Zelli, F., & van Asselt, H. (2010). The overlap between the UN climate regime and the World Trade Organization: Lessons for post-2012 climate governance. In F. Biermann, P. Pattberg, & F. Zelli, eds., *Global Climate Governance Beyond 2012: Architecture, Agency and Adaptation*. Cambridge University Press, pp. 79–96.

Zelli, F., & van Asselt, H. (2013). Introduction: The institutional fragmentation of global environmental governance: Causes, consequences, and responses. *Global Environmental Politics*, *13*, 1–13.

Zeng, K., & Eastin, J. (2012). Do developing countries invest up? The environmental effects of foreign direct investment from less-developed countries. *World Development*, *40*(11), 2221–33.

Zhou, L., Tian, X., & Zhou, Z. (2017). The effects of environmental provisions in RTAs on PM2.5 air pollution. *Applied Economics*, *49*(27), 2630–41.

Acknowledgements

This Element builds on earlier research we conducted with various co-authors. They include (in alphabetical order) Axel Berger, Zach Dove, James Hollway, Sikina Jinnah, Rakhyun Kim, Noémie Laurens, Dominique Blümer, Joost Pauwelyn, Myriam Rochette, Jakob Schwab, and Frederik Stender. They have all been insightful and diligent co-authors and we owe them for much of what we have learnt in the past few years on the interplay between trade and environment. We also want to thank the numerous and dedicated research assistants from the German Institute of Development and Sustainability (IDOS), formerly Deutsches Institut für Entwicklungspolitik (DIE) and the Canada Research Chair in International Political Economy. IDOS is grateful for financial support from the German Federal Ministry for Economic Cooperation and Development (BMZ) and the state of North Rhine-Westphalia. Last but not least, we are very grateful for the helpful comments received from three anonymous reviewers on earlier versions of this manuscript and would like to thank all colleagues, experts and friends with whom we have discussed trade and the environment over the years.

About the Authors

Clara Brandi is Head of Research Programme at the German Institute of Development and Sustainability (IDOS) and Professor of International Economics and Development Economics at the University of Bonn. She holds a PhD from the European University Institute and degrees from the University of Freiburg and Oxford University.

Jean-Frédéric Morin is Full Professor at the Political Science Department of Laval University, Canada. Before being invited by Laval University to hold the Canada Research Chair in International Political Economy, he was professor of international relations at the Free University of Brussels from 2008 to 2014 and researcher at McGill University.

Cambridge Elements ☰

Earth System Governance

Frank Biermann
Utrecht University

Frank Biermann is Research Professor of Global Sustainability Governance with the Copernicus Institute of Sustainable Development, Utrecht University, the Netherlands. He is the founding Chair of the Earth System Governance Project, a global transdisciplinary research network launched in 2009; and Editor-in-Chief of the new peer-reviewed journal *Earth System Governance* (Elsevier). In April 2018, he won a European Research Council Advanced Grant for a research program on the steering effects of the Sustainable Development Goals.

Aarti Gupta
Wageningen University

Aarti Gupta is Professor of Global Environmental Governance at Wageningen University, The Netherlands. She is Lead Faculty and a member of the Scientific Steering Committee of the Earth System Governance (ESG) Project and a Coordinating Lead Author of its 2018 Science and Implementation Plan. She is also principal investigator of the Dutch Research Council-funded TRANSGOV project on the Transformative Potential of Transparency in Climate Governance. She holds a PhD from Yale University in environmental studies.

Michael Mason
London School of Economics and Political Science

Michael Mason is a full professor in the Department of Geography and Environment at the London School of Economics and Political Science. At LSE he is also Director of the Middle East Centre and an Associate of the Grantham Institute on Climate Change and the Environment. Alongside his academic research on environmental politics and governance, he has advised various governments and international organisations on environmental policy issues, including the European Commission, ICRC, NATO, the UK Government (FCDO), and UNDP.

About the Series

Linked with the Earth System Governance Project, this exciting new series will provide concise but authoritative studies of the governance of complex socio-ecological systems, written by world-leading scholars. Highly interdisciplinary in scope, the series will address governance processes and institutions at all levels of decision-making, from local to global, within a planetary perspective that seeks to align current institutions and governance systems with the fundamental 21st Century challenges of global environmental change and earth system transformations.Elements in this series will present cutting edge scientific research, while also seeking to contribute innovative transformative ideas towards better governance. A key aim of the series is to present policy-relevant research that is of interest to both academics and policy-makers working on earth system governance.
More information about the Earth System Governance project can be found at: www.earthsystemgovernance.org.

Cambridge Elements ☰

Earth System Governance

Printed in the United States
by Baker & Taylor Publisher Services